The Art of Fashion

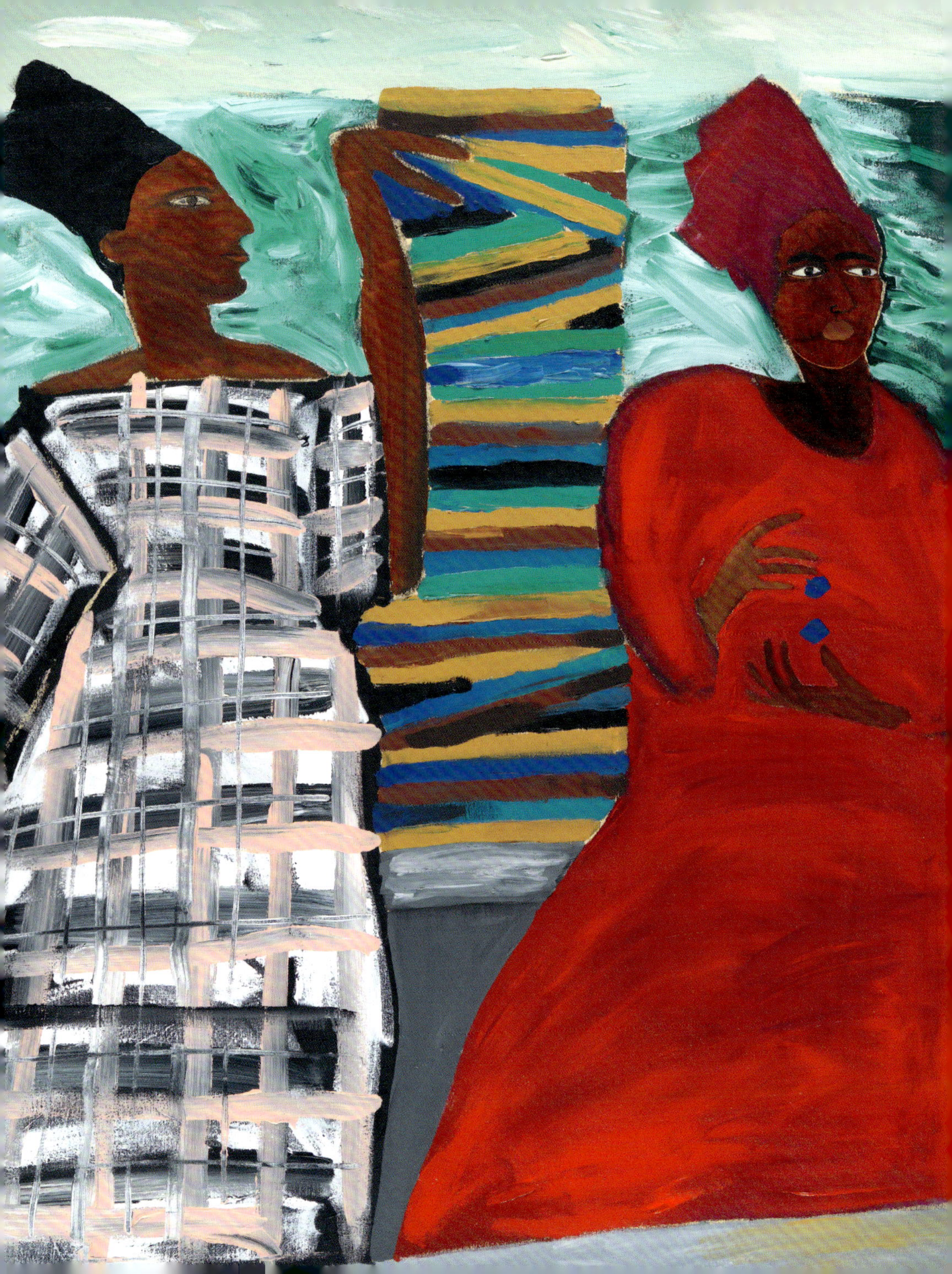

MICHAL GOLDSCHMIDT

The Art of Fashion

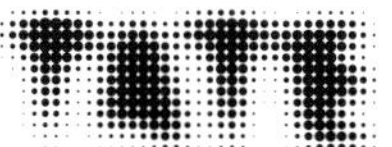

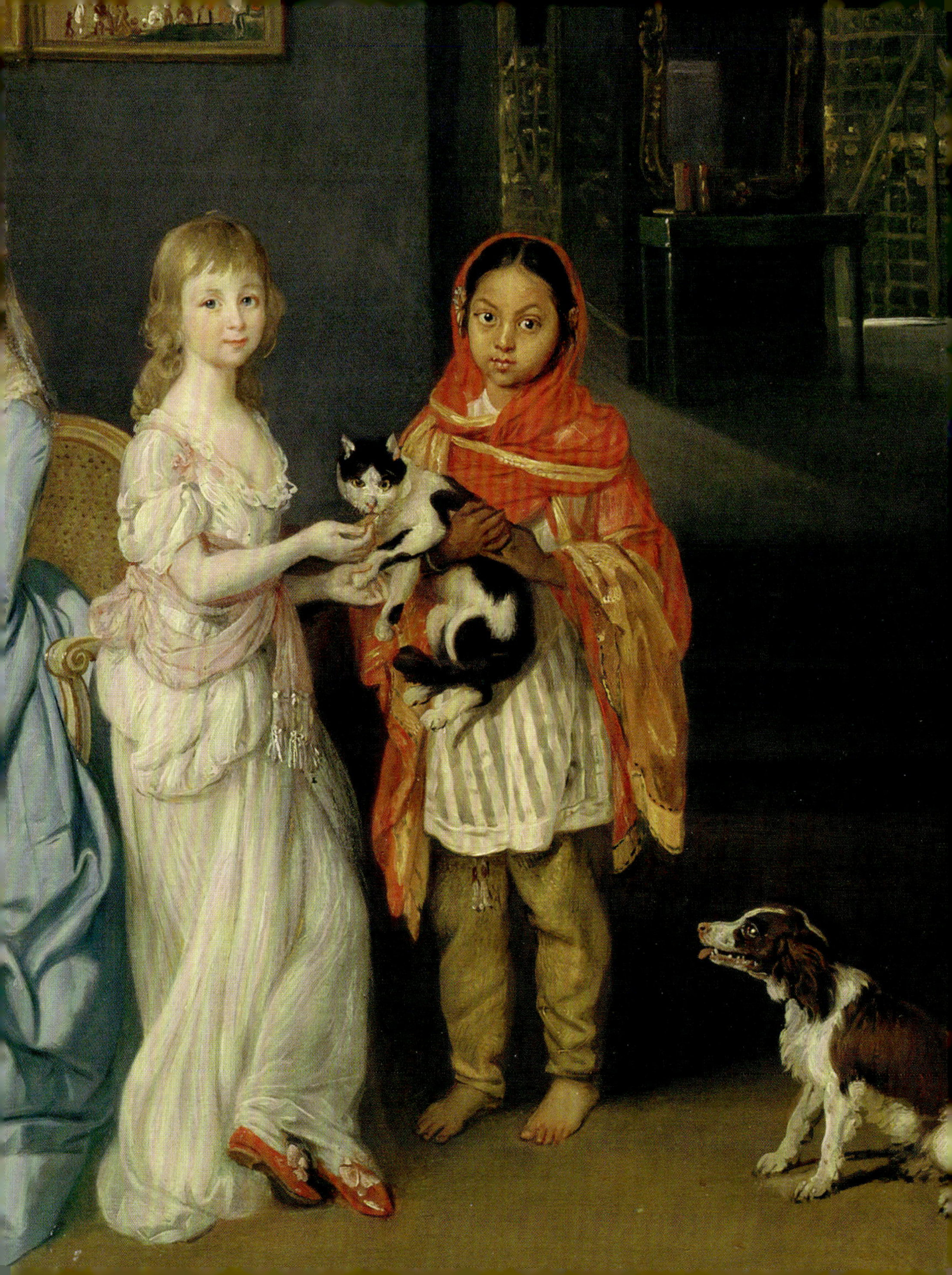

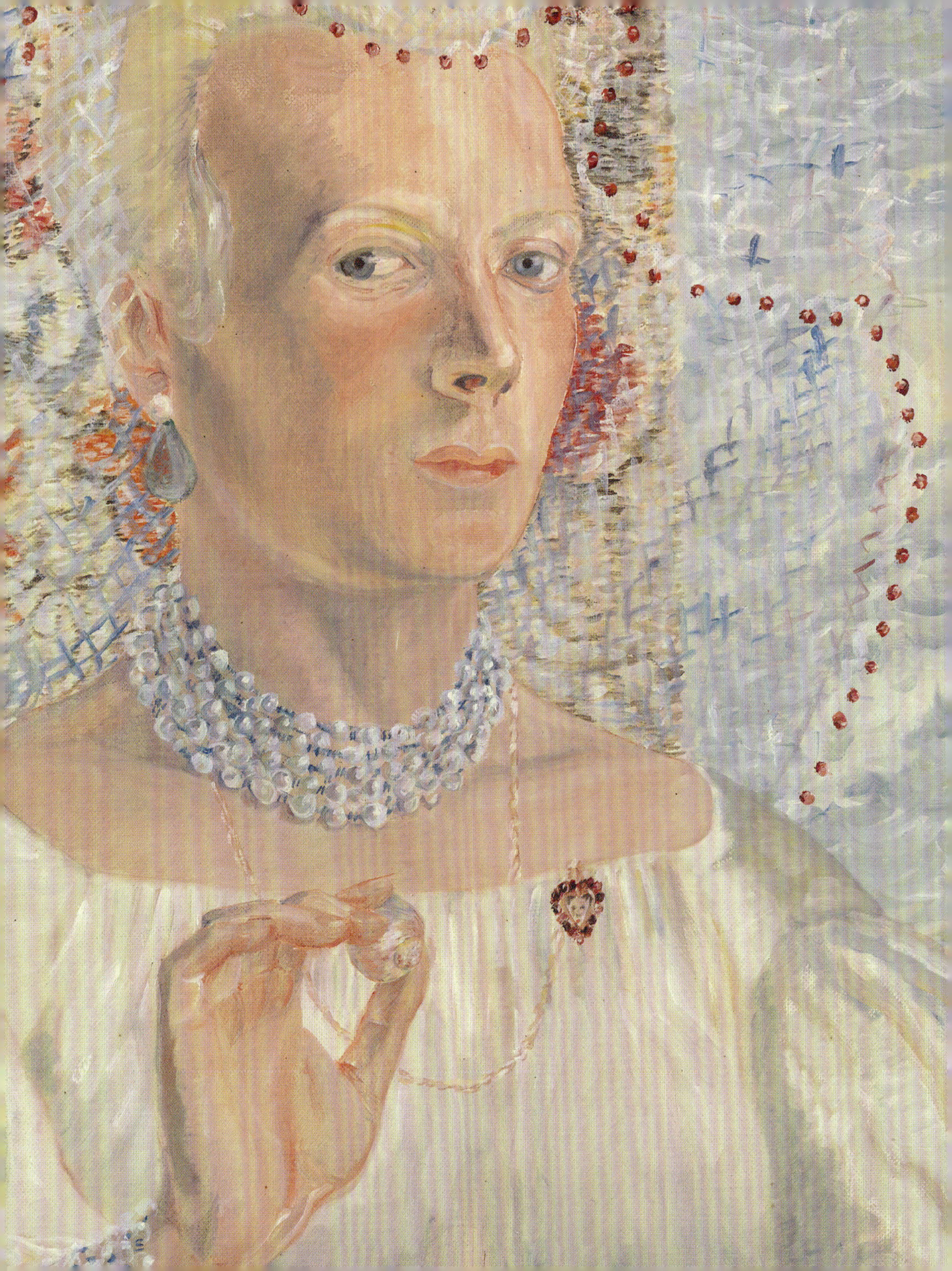

Introduction

'Fashion is the expression of society'
— Honoré de Balzac[1]

In 2004, the fashion and art press was abuzz with the news that Alexander McQueen had chosen experimental choreographer and dancer Michael Clark to choreograph his Spring/Summer catwalk show. Though a dancer, Clark's work was already blurring the boundaries of traditional categorisations: after he began a collaboration with British artist Sarah Lucas in 2001 with *Before and After: The Fall*, many thought of his dance choreography and installations as being at the forefront of cutting-edge contemporary performance art. McQueen's choice of Clark indicated a desire for his own art to join the mix in a similar manner. Held at the Salle Wagram, a nineteenth-century Parisian ballroom turned concert hall, McQueen's 2004 show abstractly enacted the plot of the 1969 film *They Shoot Horses, Don't They?* McQueen's models moved according to a choreography of Clark's devising, wearing the clothing of McQueen's imagination as they recreated a pre-existing commercial film. In its very interdisciplinary nature, McQueen's show argued for the interdependent nature of different forms of art and the world of couture seasonal fashion of which he was part. It is time, McQueen was saying, to consider the creative repercussions fashion has had on forms of high art.

But the relationship between the world of seasonal high fashion and art is nothing new. Indeed, since the initial emergence of fashion houses, seasonal shows and department stores in the late nineteenth century, the two have existed in a uniquely symbiotic relationship. In couture's birthplace, Paris, the redesign of its neighbourhoods and widening of its

Sylvia Sleigh *The Bride (Lawrence Alloway)* 1949 (detail, see p.141)

central boulevards by Georges-Eugène Haussmann quite literally paved the way for the development of new types of real estate in the centre of the city. The urban landscape shifted concurrently with Aristide Boucicaut's redesign and expansion of Le Bon Marché, giving rise to concentrated central shopping districts in which followers of fashion could shop while being observed wearing the latest trends.

The impressionists were particularly fascinated by this turn of events and, seeing the fashionable Parisienne as a key character of sophisticated modernity, set about depicting her in their paintings. Where the earlier French realists had fixated on the character, clothing and activities of the rural working classes, Édouard Manet and his circle documented the rapidly transforming trimmings of the urban upper classes, obsessively and accurately depicting the up-to-the-minute fashion trends of the capital in their paintings. From the beginning, then, modern art and modern fashion took note of one another.

This artistic acknowledgement of fashion's cultural implications continued apace throughout the twentieth century. In Vienna in 1905, Josef Hoffmann and Koloman Moser, key members of the design collective The Wiener Werkstätte, started arguing for the importance of wearing clothing that reflected their aesthetic. In 1910, the collective launched their own fashion department to produce textile designs and accessories. When the group of London artists known as the Bloomsbury Group launched their Omega Workshop collective under the direction of Roger Fry in 1913, they included textile and clothing designs among their offerings. In Italy the following year, futurist Giacomo Balla published *Le Vêtement Masculin Futuriste: Manifeste*, in which he argued that the futurists' principles of industrial dynamism and efficiency should be expanded to be applied to clothing. In Russia, constructivists Alexander Rodchenko and Natalia Goncharova designed overalls consisting of the clean, simple geometric shapes they used for their artworks. The Ukrainian artist Sonia Delaunay's Paris studio was the site of her creation of colourful, abstract 'simultaneous' works – both textile designs and artworks at the same time. By the second decade of the twentieth century, Delaunay already saw her artistic and textile design practice as an intertwined and interdisciplinary project ahead of its time.

At the same time, fashion designers and couture houses were also turning to artists for their creative development. In Paris, master couturier Paul Poiret commissioned fauvist painter Raoul Dufy to design textiles for him to use in his collections. Fashion designer Jean Patou commissioned Lázsló Moholy-Nagy, then a professor at the Bauhaus, to create fabrics for him that reflected the Hungarian artist's constructivist outlook. Perhaps most famously, Elsa Schiaparelli collaborated with many key European artists as part of her fashion output, including Cecil Beaton, Jean Cocteau, Alberto Giacometti and Man Ray. In 1938, Schiaparelli and Salvador Dalí collaborated to create her label's Tears dress: a pale-blue viscose rayon, the sheath dress featured Dalí's magenta paintings of ripped fabric repeating across the garment. Schiaparelli was most likely inspired to create the dress with Dalí by his earlier painting *Three Young Surrealist Women Holding in their Arms the Skins of an Orchestra* 1936, in which the middle figure wears a dress with tears in it, resembling Schiaparelli's ultimate creation. Presented as part of a dramatically acrobatic collection and show she called *Circus*, Schiaparelli and Dalí's Tears dress offered a moment of sober reflection on the geopolitical situation of the age, an artistic moment of reflection in the form of apparel.

Many fashion houses continue this spirit of collaboration today, boldly and prominently broadcasting their relationships with the hottest and most commercially appealing global artists. The flagship Tokyo branch of Commes des Garçons has hosted numerous exhibitions of contemporary artists, including Daniel Buren and Cindy Sherman. In 2000, designer Helmut Lang commissioned American artist Jenny Holzer to create a poster work to celebrate the launch of his fragrance.

In 2023, Louis Vuitton's collaboration with Yayoi Kusama sold out rapidly within days of each new product launch. Artistic collaboration seems to be fruitful for fashion houses. Many artists, meanwhile, underplay the role of fashion in the work they create as part of their personal oeuvre: while Kusama may give over her likeness to statues in Louis Vuitton stores around the world, her collaborative pieces are decidedly accessories, not part of her artistic output. Likewise, while Holzer's collaboration with Lang took on the aesthetic and mode of her *Living* series, it is not listed as part of that work on her official website. It seems that in the twenty-first century, to an extent, the creative juices are only fully acknowledged as flowing in one direction.

This book aims to explore that permeable boundary between the two disciplines, taking specific works as case studies of this interplay. Spanning the nineteenth, twentieth and twenty-first centuries, it looks at the different ways modern art and modern fashion have informed the creation of these works in individual and idiosyncratic ways. The book is divided into six thematic chapters, which look at the different ways that fashion features or is used in these works. The first chapter, 'Colonial Clothing', takes a critical approach to the role of empires, colonialism and trade in the shaping of modern fashion and art. 'In Vogue' looks at the role of fashion magazines, fashion plates and print culture in the formation of fashion, trends and the resultant selected artworks. In 'Uniform Style' the role of uniforms – of both the voluntary and mandatory types – in fashion is analysed. 'Swinging Sixties' looks at the ways the transformational subcultures of the 1960s were reflected by the art of its time, while 'Street Style' considers the resultant interest in individual fashions and teen clans in the media and art. Finally, 'Fashioning the Self' considers the ways artists have presented themselves sartorially to the public and the key role of timely fashions in the cultivation of an artistic persona.

 Gwen John *Self-Portrait* 1902 (detail, see p.137)

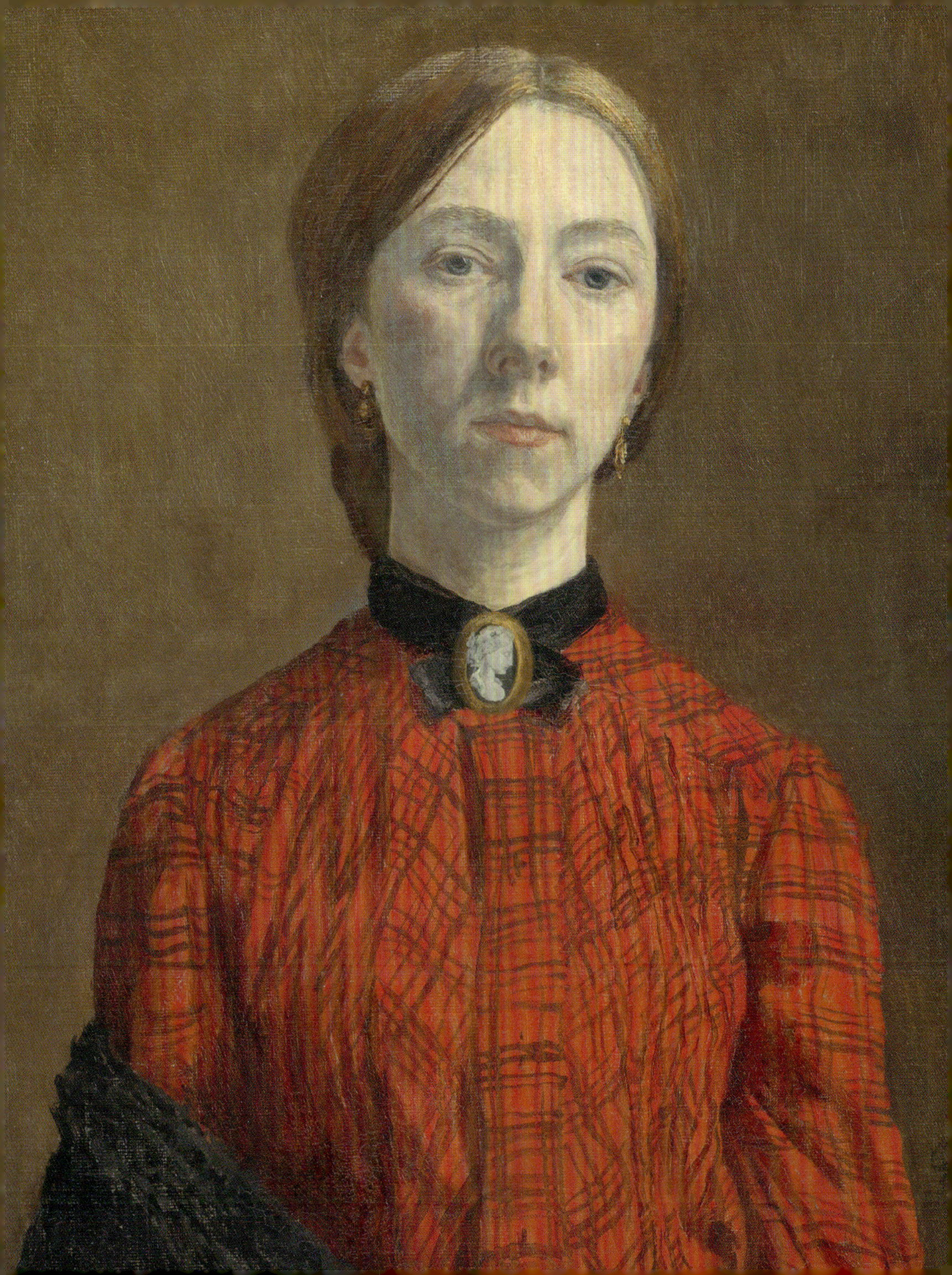

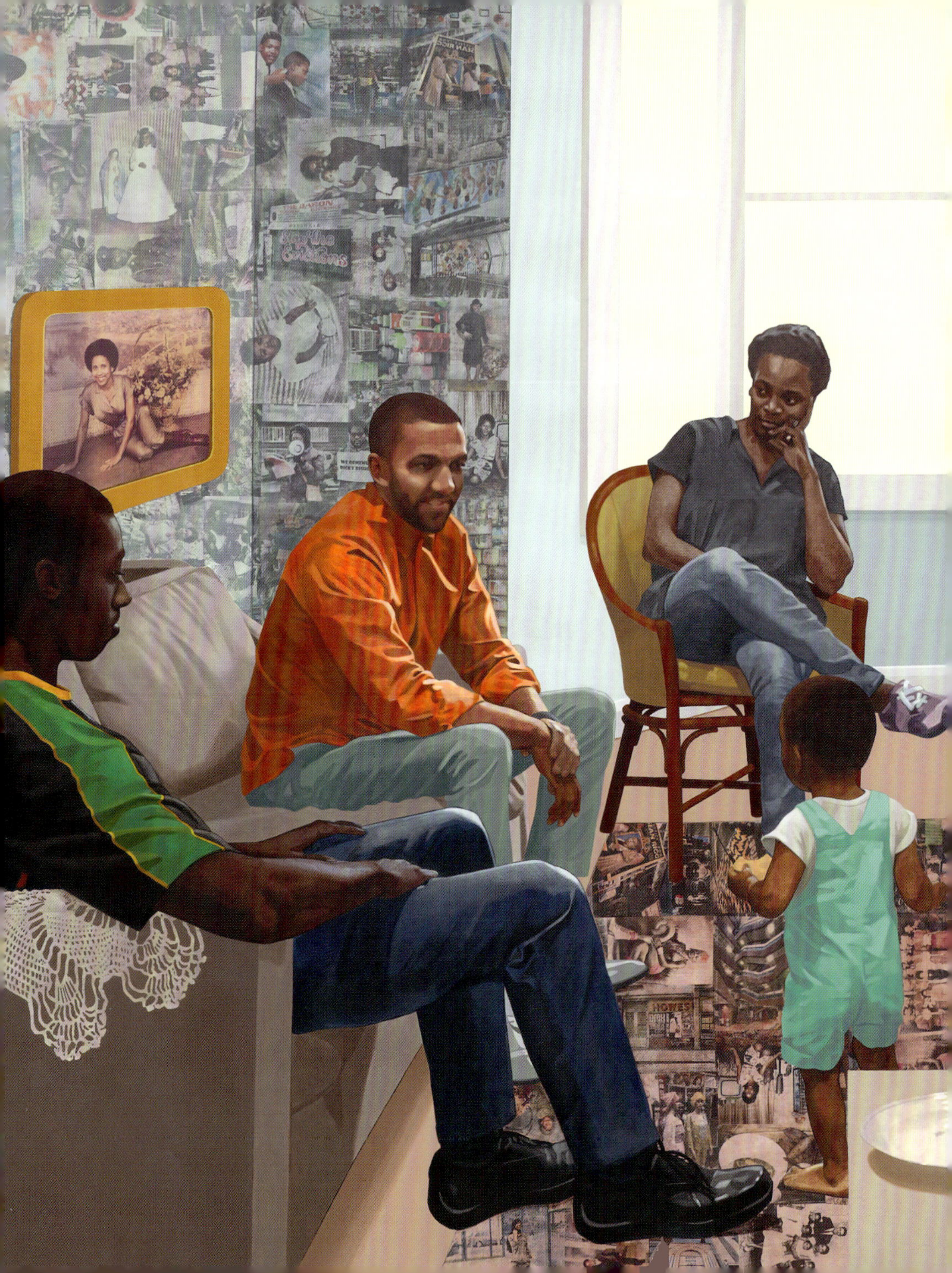

Colonial Clothing

Countries in the Global South with fewer human rights protections and factory safeguarding measures, such as China and India, currently manufacture the majority of the world's clothing. In these countries, reduced oversight of working conditions and lower wages than are provided at factories in the Global North combine with less restrictive environmental laws regarding which chemicals can and cannot be used in the production process to enable factories to produce garments for significantly lower prices than their Global Northern competitors. This in turn fuels the desire for mass consumption of affordable garments. In spite of a backlash against the culture of 'fast fashion' that has led to the current iteration of this dynamic, wealthy nations' reliance upon less economically developed countries for textiles is nothing new.

For hundreds of years, the Western textiles from which sartorial fashions are created have been reliant upon colonial trade networks at their very core. The development of the Atlantic Slave Trade saw slave-labour-powered cotton plantations in the Americas supplying many of the textiles found in Europe and North America. After the British East India Company received its Royal Charter from Elizabeth I in 1600, cotton from India was also imported to England. Until the late eighteenth century, when 'Company governments' were established in the region, the British only had access to more crude muslin textiles; after overthrowing the Mughal Court, who had traditionally reserved the finest muslins for themselves, the British could trade in higher quality fabrics, too, as Indian textile production was now under their control. Both the quality of the cotton and the method of weaving it were far superior to anything the British could achieve for themselves, and a large part of the East India Company's revenue came from exported Indian cotton.

In 1853, Japan ended its policy of isolationism, allowing visitors to its shores and commencing global trade at unprecedented levels. Many in the West were fascinated by anything that could illustrate the traditions and aesthetics of a country that had been shrouded in mystery for so long. Cloth could

 Page 12: Njideka Akunyili Crosby *Remain, Thriving* 2018 (detail, see pp.34–5)

be transported easily and cheaply from Japan, and embroidered Japanese textiles became many nineteenth-century Westerners' first encounter with Japanese culture.

In many East African countries, high-quality cloth was a marker of prestige, wealth and sophistication; this notion spread even further when Dutch textiles manufacturers started producing batik-inspired textiles (now known as 'Dutch Wax') on an industrial scale and selling them to inhabitants of the Gold Coast.

This section looks at artworks where the featured fabrics rely on distinct colonial pathways, where modes of dress serve to highlight those who belong and those who do not, and where the enduring impact of colonialism rears its head in unexpected ways.

Johan Zoffany 1733–1810
Colonel Blair with his Family and an Indian Ayah 1786
Oil paint on canvas 124.7 × 163.5

In both activity and dress, Colonel Blair's daughters and wife demonstrate their Western feminine virtue. One girl sits before sheet music, demonstrating her proficiency in a Western musical tradition seen as an acceptable pursuit for a noblewoman. The Colonel's wife sits holding his hand, her other hand in her lap as she gazes at him – a portrait of wifely devotion. Although the younger daughter stands with her back to the family, she faces the animals in the image, her devotion to them (and theirs to her) an indication of her nurturing personality. Within the composition, Zoffany uses dress to differentiate the background and subsequent status of the sitters, enhancing the dissimilarity between the family and the Indian girl who stands in the corner of the work.

During the eighteenth century, Western children of the upper classes often wore white to reflect their innocence relative to the adults around them, just as Colonel Blair's younger daughter does here. In direct contrast, the Indian girl wears a richly embroidered red and gold dupatta around her shoulders and hair, and a striped white kameez that appears to be made from striped alacha cloth, over khaki churidar. Calico, muslin and other specialty Bengali textiles were among the main sources of the East India Company's profits throughout the seventeenth and eighteenth centuries. Though Zoffany's scene firmly places the family in India, their choice of Western dress and fabrics demonstrates their desire not to engage fully with the very goods that have made them wealthy.

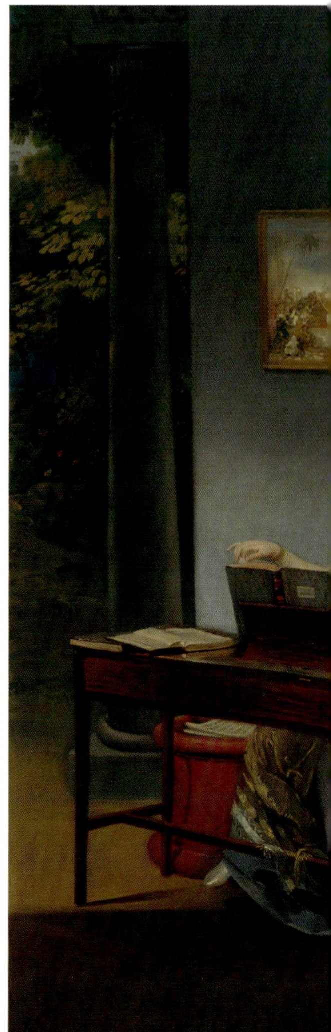

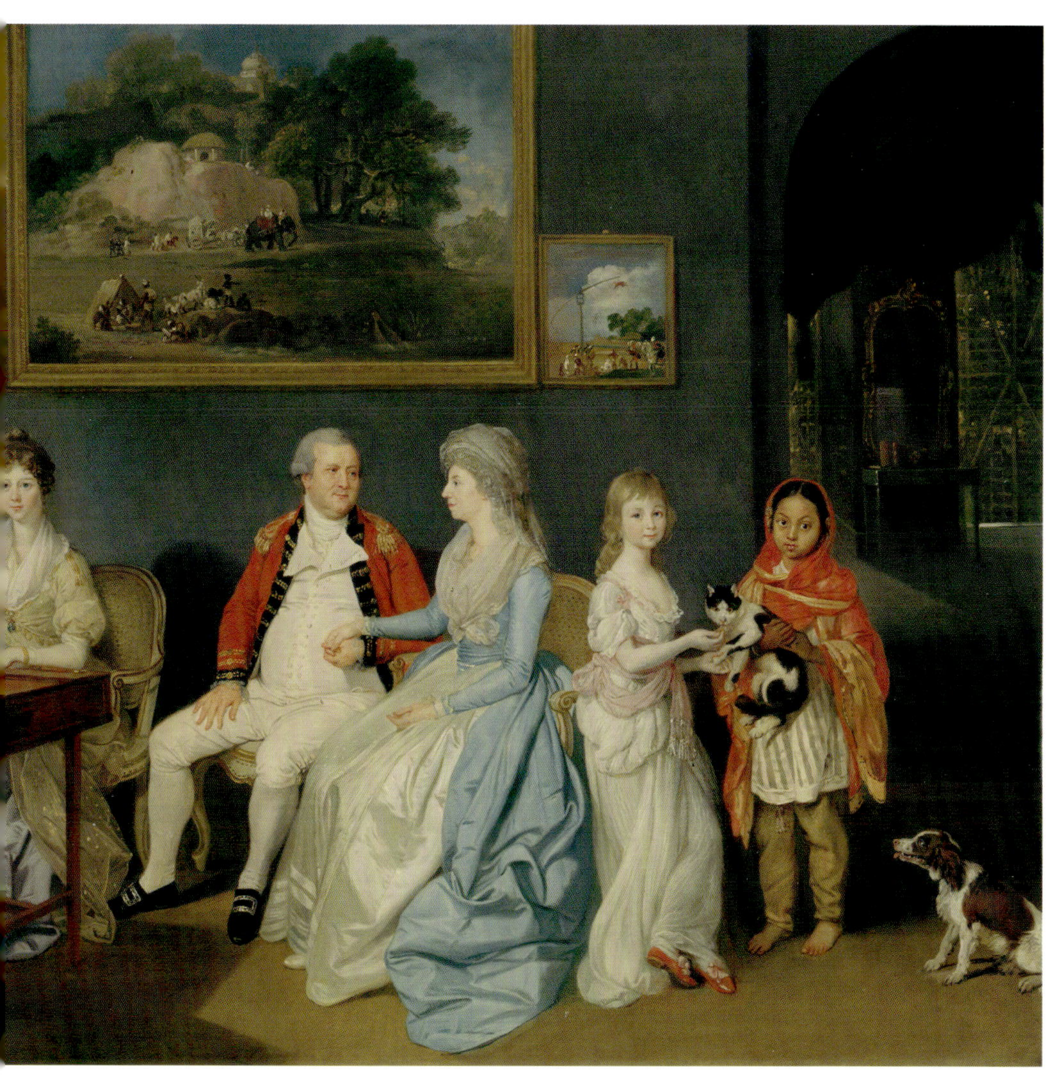

Dante Gabriel Rossetti 1828–82
Monna Vanna 1866
Oil paint on canvas 88.9 × 86.4

Rossetti's *Monna Vanna* presents a luxuriously decorated sitter who glows as sumptuously as her clothing. A long string of bright red coral loops around her neck several times, interweaving with the large pendant that hangs from her tight gold choker. Pearl spiral clips keep her large masses of red locks from her face. Other gold and emerald embellishments are sprinkled across the canvas. In direct contrast to the Victorian fashion for tightly corseted torsos, cinched waists and hooped crinoline skirts, Rossetti's model wears a loose-fitting dress with puffed sleeves. The fabric is richly embroidered in the style of art needlework, a form of freehand embroidery revived by William Morris in the latter half of the nineteenth century.

The way Rossetti and other members of his artistic circle, the Pre-Raphaelite Brotherhood, dressed their models quickly caught on, and soon many women in England were wearing 'artistic' dress. By using art – rather than fashion houses, fashion plates and women's publications – as a mode of reference for their wardrobe, these women could feel they were engaging in a higher pursuit that marked them as more sophisticated than others. The corset-less, loose style became popular with intellectuals, artists and artists' wives. Many of the materials were dyed using traditional techniques, which, coupled with hand embroidery, made a distinct anti-industrialisation statement. Wearing artistic dress also signified a distinct appreciation for artisanal skill and traditional English handicraft, and an affinity with Morris and his campaign to preserve the traditional forms of craftsmanship.

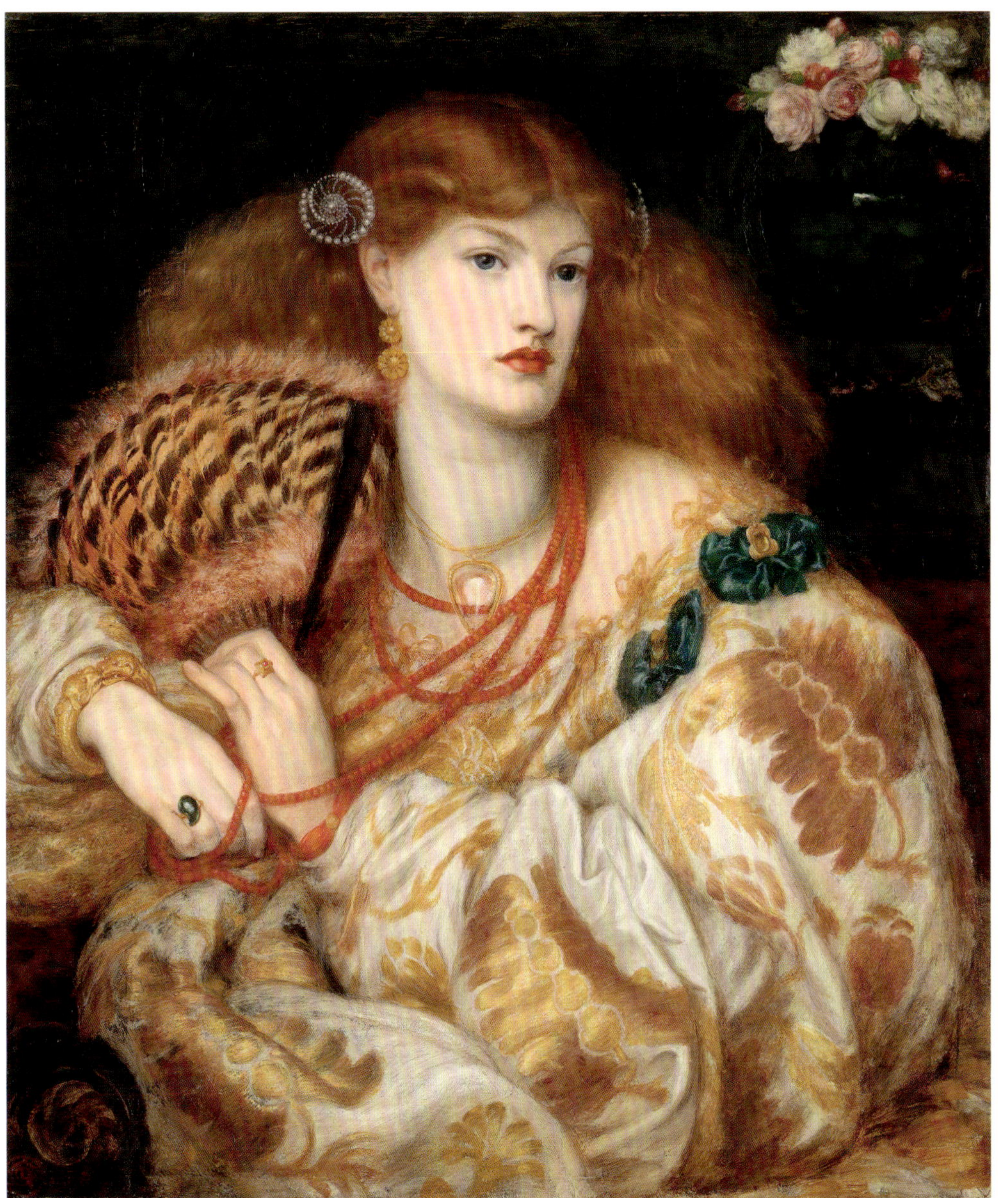

Julia Margaret Cameron 1815–79
Rebecca c.1870
Albumen print 45.2 × 35.9 (with mount)

Cameron was one of the first photographers to use photography – a new medium that recreated things in a manner people felt was 'truthful' or 'accurate' – for imaginary and fanciful ends. Here, Cameron creates a moody vignette of the Biblical figure Rebecca lost in thought and shrouded in a mystical haze. In the tale of Rebecca, recounted in the book of Genesis, Rebecca proves herself worthy of marrying Abraham's son Isaac when she offers his servant, Elijah, water for both himself and his camels.

Cameron dresses her Rebecca in an idiosyncratic manner. She covers her hair with a patterned shawl, secured by a row of woven discs that tie across her forehead. Though blurred and out of focus, the material covering the model's head appears to be paisley, an ornamental curved textile pattern woven into the fabric, rather than embroidered or printed on the textile later. This style was based upon early nineteenth-century shawls brought back by businessmen and returning members of the East India Company after trips to Kashmir, where they found densely patterned shawls. Factories in the Scottish town of Paisley worked out how to replicate a similar design and effect using industrial machines, thereby creating a cheaper product that could undercut the original imported from abroad. Though now manufactured in Scotland, the style was still associated with India, and the East more generally, by a Victorian culture that was not particularly interested in differentiating between the many distinct non-Western nations they were interacting with at an unprecedented level. As one of the matriarchs of the Hebrew Bible, Rebecca is often thought of as a quintessentially Jewish woman. Cameron's use of a paisley fabric in her presentation of Rebecca may have been a means to signify her status as non-Western or an attempt to recreate a costume Cameron felt would have been worn by an ancient Canaanite.

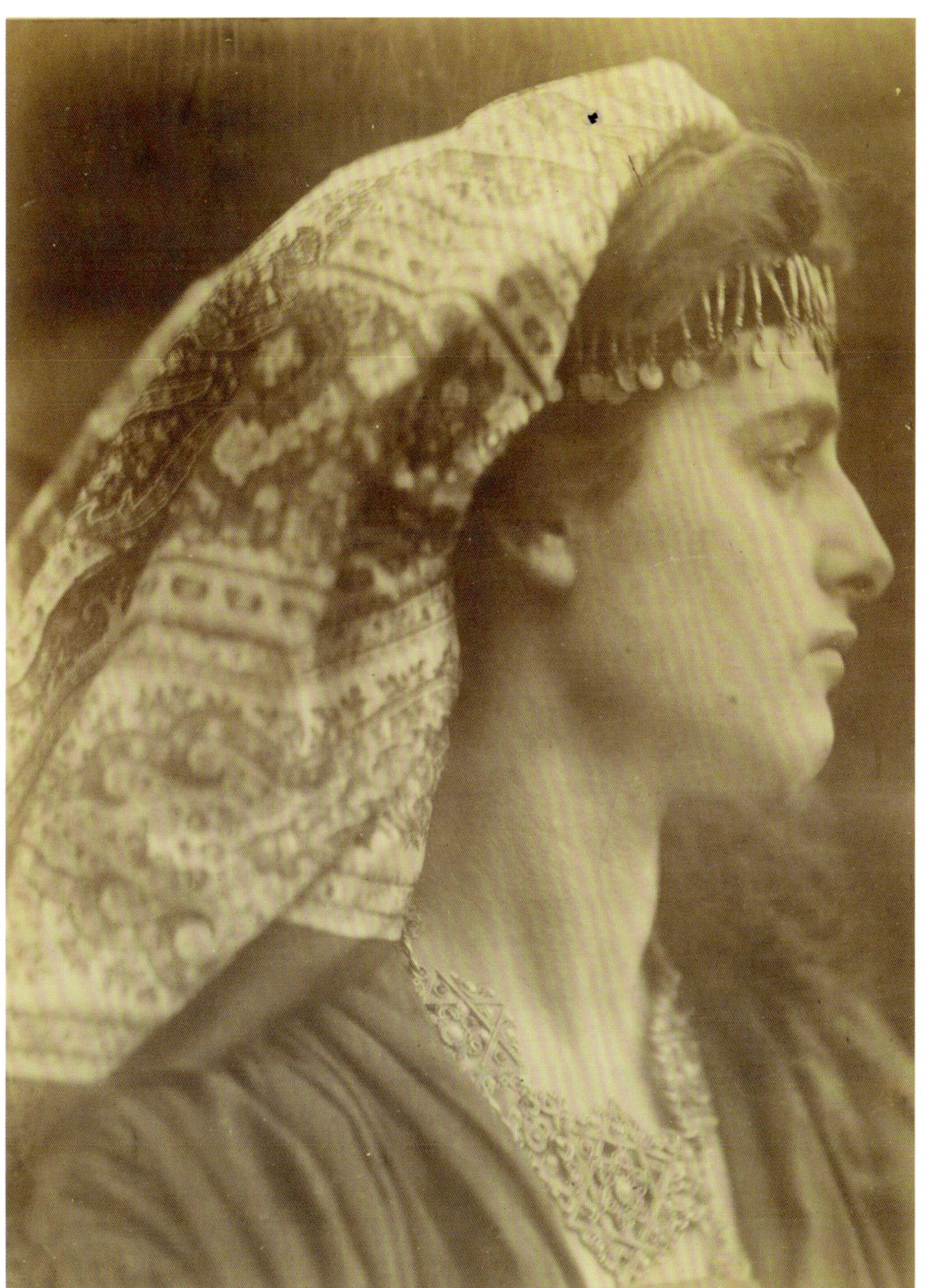

Max Beerbohm 1872–1956
Rossetti, having just had a fresh consignment of 'stunning' fabrics ... tries hard to prevail on his younger sister to accept ... one 1917
Part of *Rossetti and his Friends*
Graphite and watercolour on paper 34.3 × 28.6

In this cartoon, Beerbohm pokes fun at Dante Gabriel Rossetti's participation in the Victorian craze for fabrics imported from non-Western countries. After the end of Japanese isolationism in 1853, clear channels of communication and trade opened up between Japan and much of Western Europe. This, coupled with the increasing colonial presence of the British in India, led to a boom in the trade of non-Western fabrics, particularly to Scotland, England and France. Prominent artists of the time such as Édouard Manet, Mary Cassatt and Rossetti felt inspired by the Japanese art that was arriving in Europe. Aesthetic elements and details were widely adapted and used in Western painting, furniture design, fashion and interior design. The extent of Japan's influence in the cultural arenas of many Western countries is often called *japonisme*.

In London, department store Liberty & Co. was one of the main drivers of the craze. Arthur Lasenby Liberty founded the store in 1875 originally as an Eastern Bazaar, stocking textiles and a selection of trinkets from Japan, India and China. Liberty imported its wares directly, and the unpacking of a new shipment in store was an occasion that drew crowds of curious onlookers. In this cartoon, Rossetti and one of his sisters stand in a room in which many coloured fabrics are draped over a motley arrangement of chairs. The caption in full reads 'Rossetti, having just had a fresh consignment of "stunning" fabrics from that new shop in Regent Street, tries hard to prevail on his younger sister to accept at any rate one of these and have a dress made of it from designs to be furnished by himself.'[2] The implication is clear: swept up in the colonial craze for Eastern fabrics, Rossetti is feeling inspired by the newly arrived collection of fabrics he has just purchased from Liberty & Co.

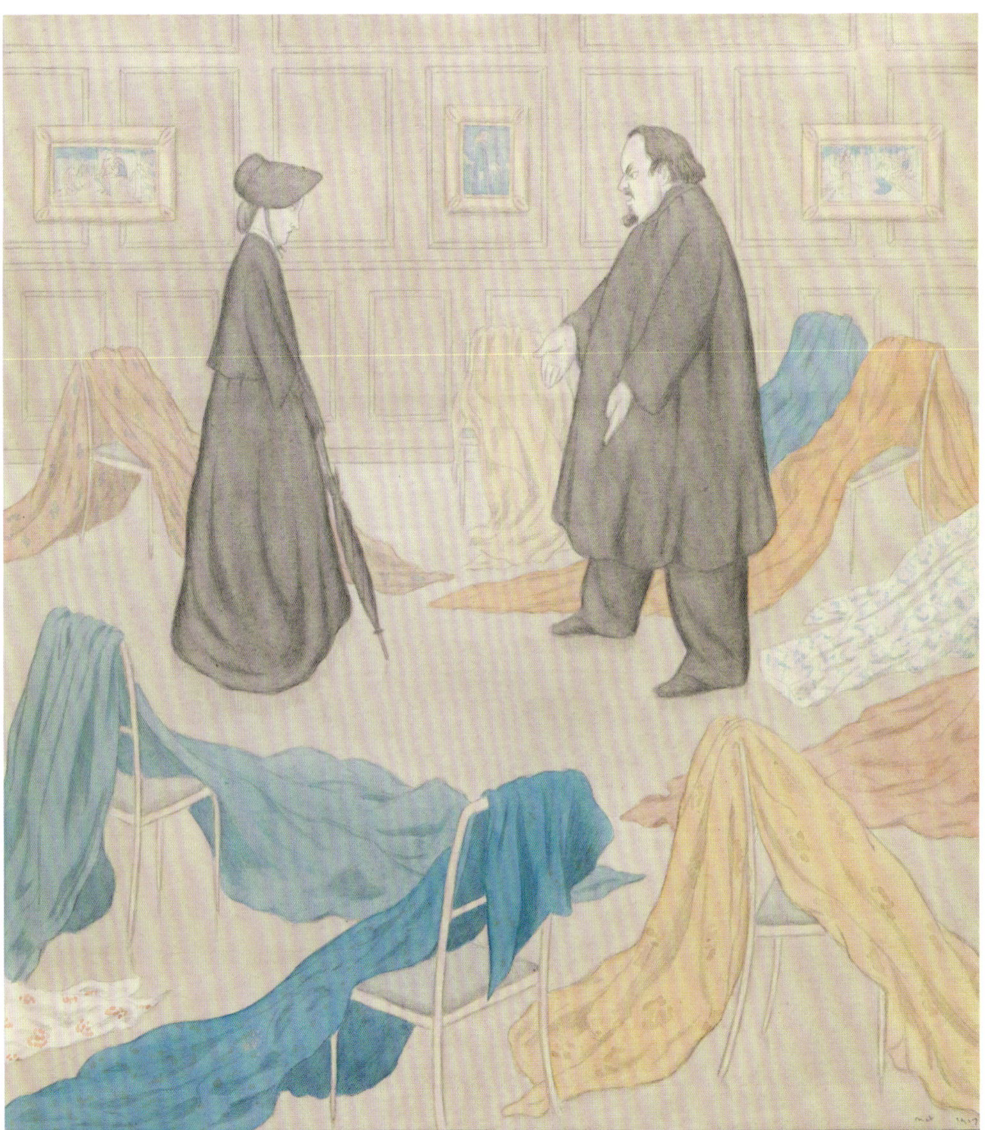

Rossetti, having just had a fresh consignment of "stunning" fabrics from that new shop in Regent Street, tries hard to prevail on his younger sister to accept at any rate one of these and have a dress made of it from designs to be furnished by himself.

D. G. R. "What *is* the use, Christina, of having a heart like a singing-bird and a water-shoot and all the rest of it, if you insist on getting yourself up like a pew-opener?"

C. R. "Well, Gabriel, I don't know; I'm sure you yourself always dress very simply."

Dora Maar 1907–97
Pearly King collecting money for the Empire Day 1935
Gelatin silver print on paper 27.3 × 23.5

In this image, French photographer Dora Maar captures two uniquely British phenomena: Pearly Kings and Empire Day. From the late nineteenth century until the 1950s, one day a year was designated Empire Day across the British Empire. The British presence throughout myriad different territories across the globe was celebrated on this (inter)national holiday.

Maar's photograph is taken from a low angle, causing the light and the emphasis of the image to fall on the unique clothing her subject is wearing. The man's flat cap and suit jacket are embroidered with mother-of-pearl buttons of various shapes and sizes and in different configurations, marking him as a 'Pearly King' – a person who would collect on behalf of a local charity fund known as a 'Pearly' Guild or Association. Given the increased footfall in the city's streets on Empire Day, members of London Pearly charities made sure they were out collecting money for their good causes. The custom of wearing such an outfit for collecting arose from the charity's originator, nineteenth-century road sweeper Henry Croft. Towards the end of the century Britain was swept up in a craze for mother-of pearl buttons, sparked by the rich supply of the material that was to be found in the colonial outpost of Broome, Western Australia. Those who worked on London's streets as costermongers or street sweepers would collect the beautiful buttons that fell off expensive coats, sewing them onto their own clothing as ornamentation. Croft took this trend to the extreme, covering his entire outfit with mother-of-pearl buttons to draw attention to his charitable collecting efforts. Members who came after him dressed in his honour and, in the case of Maar's image, marked Empire Day with a sartorial tradition unwittingly born of Empire.

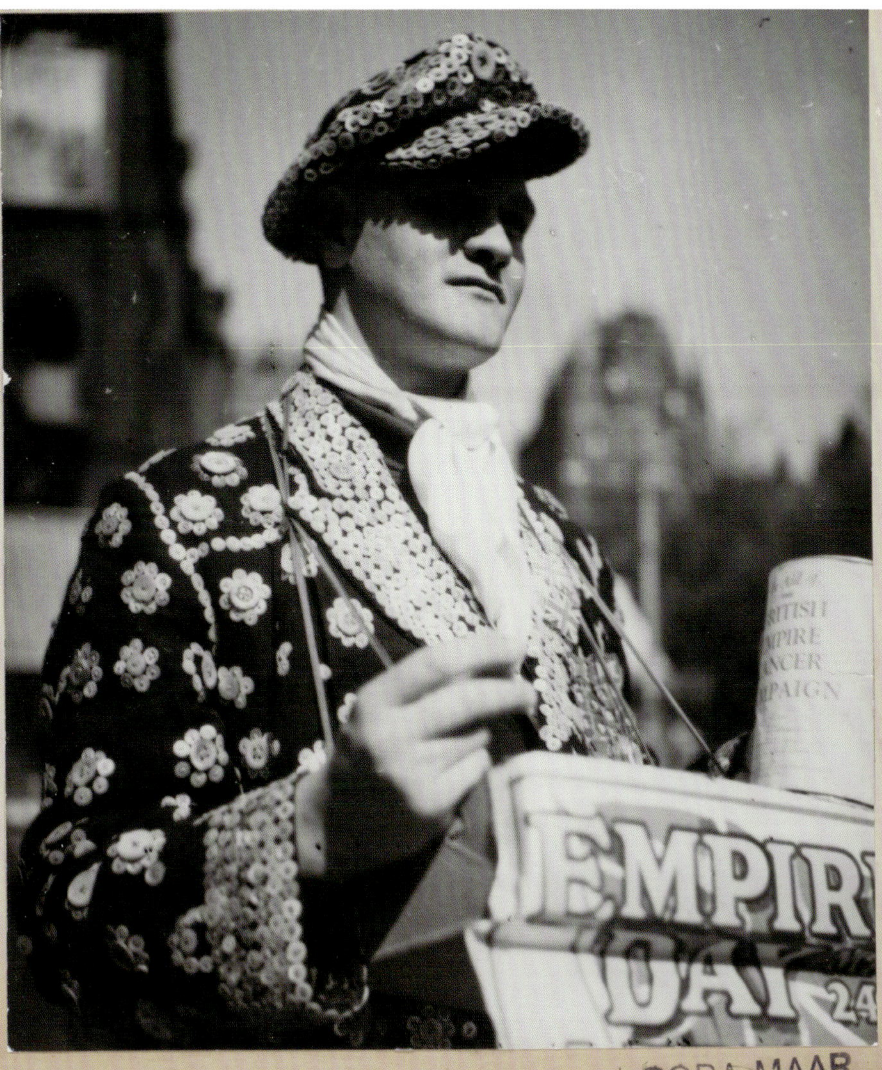
RITISH
MPIRE
NCER
PAIGN
EMPIR
DA
24
DORA MAAR

Amrita Sher-Gil 1913–41
Sumair 1936
Oil paint on canvas 91.6 × 56.5

Born to a Punjabi Sikh father and Hungarian Jewish mother, Amrita Sher-Gil was brought up between the two countries. After completing her art education at the École des Beaux-Arts in Paris, she decided to return to India to live full time and embark on her life's ambition to become a truly Indian modern painter. For Sher-Gil, her return to India was filtered through her experiences abroad. She wrote to her mother:

> Our long stay in Europe has aided me to *discover*, as it were, India. Modern Art has led me to the comprehension and appreciation of Indian painting and sculpture. It seems paradoxical, but I know for certain, that had we not come away to Europe, I should perhaps never have realized that a fresco from Ajanta or a small piece of sculpture in the Musée Guimet is worth more than the whole Renaissance!

In *Sumair*, the title an Arabic term for close friend, Sher-Gil depicts her cousin looking to one side, away from the viewer, with an intent but melancholy expression. She wears an ornately decorated green sari and beaded turquoise earrings – in some Indian traditions, turquoise is believed to promote good health and ward off the evil eye. She also wears red nail polish. Modern liquid nail polish was invented in 1917 and in 1932 Revlon released the first opaque red nail polish in the United States, sparking a craze. The technology soon spread to Europe. In India, however, women had been dying their nails using henna for centuries and, by including the red nails in this portrait, Sher-Gil allows the origin of the trend to remain ambiguous, bringing a beautiful fusion of European and Indian cosmetic fashions to the work.

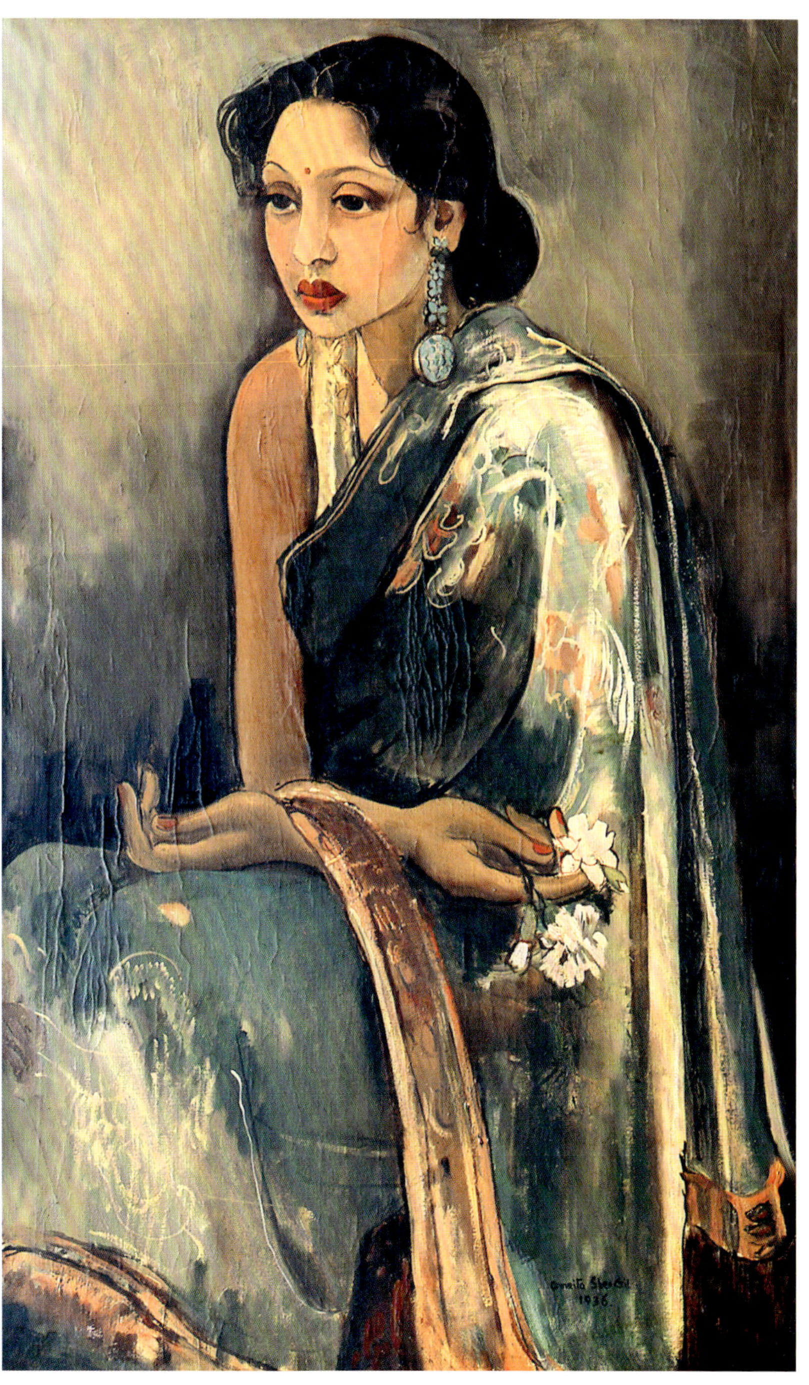
1936

Lubaina Himid 1954–
Between the Two my Heart is Balanced 1991
Acrylic paint on canvas 121.8 × 152.4

In this painting, Lubaina Himid creates a modern and more personal take on James Tissot's *Entre les deux mon coeur Balance* 1877. In Tissot's painting, a soldier sits between two women on a small boat taking them to shore from a larger ship in the distance. Both women are dressed in distinctly Victorian clothing that uses a lot of fabric draped, pleated and cut to create an abundance of frills and flounces in their skirts and sleeves. Atop their heads, their hats are worn at a tilt and their hair draws up at the back, as was the fashion in 1870s England. Himid's corresponding women wear recognisably twentieth-century African dress – long, loose straight dresses with long sleeves, cut in a bright or printed fabric – and cover their hair with fabric head wraps.

Interestingly, the woman on the left is wearing a dress that seems to be made from a checked gingham, a fabric not usually associated with the fashion of any country on the African continent. Gingham originated in sixteenth-century Dutch-occupied Malaysia as a specialty woven fabric whose Malay name, *genggang*, was changed to 'gingham' by non-Malay speakers. Through their Dutch ties, the East India Company began to export gingham fabric to England, Scotland and Wales, as well as other territories they had colonised. Himid was born in Zanzibar, Tanzania, and moved to England at a young age. Unlike the rest of Tanzania, which was occupied by Germany in the early twentieth century, Zanzibar was under British colonial rule from the late nineteenth century. If the work is interpreted as a reflection on Himid's migratory journey or those of others like her, then the inclusion of gingham fabric may be a nod to the impact of British presence and trading in the region.

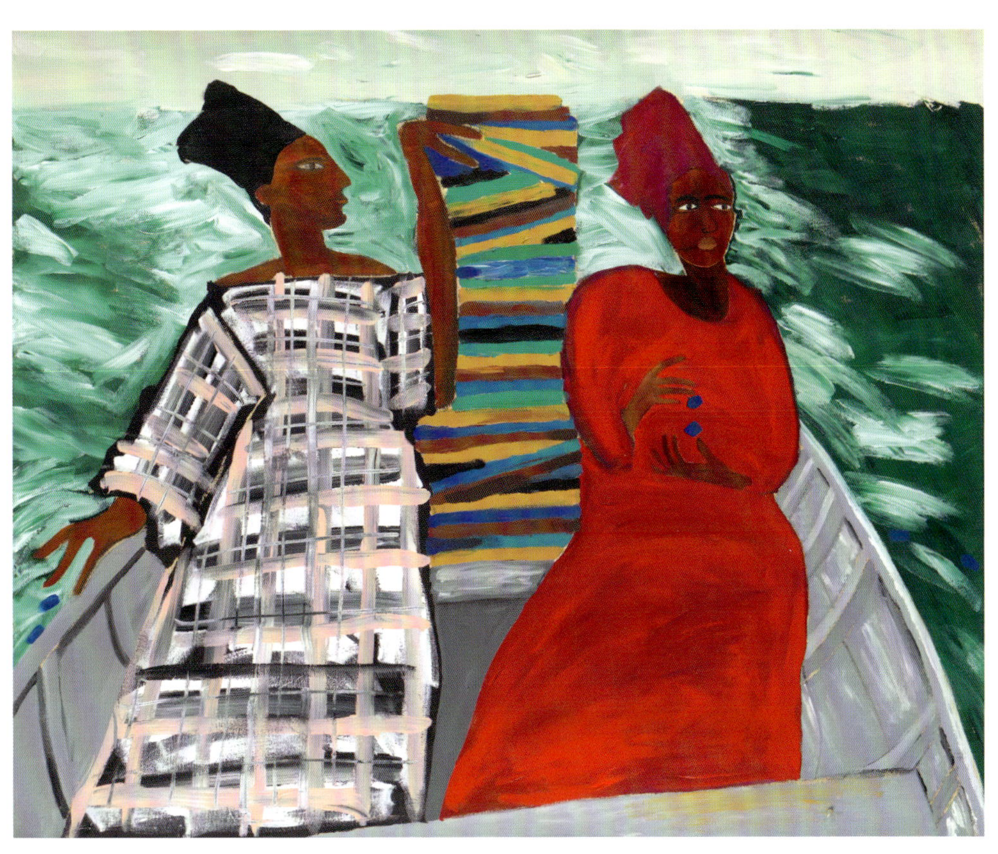

Yinka Shonibare 1962–
The Swing (after Fragonard) 2001
Mannequin, cotton costume, 2 slippers, swing seat, 2 ropes, oak twig and artificial foliage 330 × 350 × 220

Yinka Shonibare's sculpture responds to and transforms Jean-Honoré Fragonard's painting *The Swing* c.1767–8, a well-known work of the Rococo period of art. In Fragonard's original, a woman is pushed on a swing in a large garden while a man in the bushes beneath her peers up her skirt. On her head sits a wide-brimmed hat with a low crown – a bergère hat, also called a shepherdess hat. The hat was originally worn by women working on farms. In the eighteenth century, the fashion for pastoral dressing spread to French upper-class women.

In Shonibare's *The Swing (after Fragonard)*, however, not only is his swinging woman not wearing a hat, she is entirely decapitated. Instead of a pink and white silk ruched open gown with matching petticoats and lace frills, Shonibare renders the lines of his subject's clothing in Dutch Wax fabric. These fabrics originally came about when nineteenth-century Dutch businessman Pieter Fentener van Vlissingen decided to create textiles based on Indonesian batik patterns using industrial, rather than traditional, methods of production. Van Vlissingen intended the fabrics for export from the outset, and although he initially planned to sell them back to the country that provided his inspiration – Indonesia – the fabrics took off in another Dutch-occupied territory: the Gold Coast, or modern day Ghana. Over time, production moved to Ghana and the fabrics became popular in other countries in the African continent, particularly during many of the West African Independence movements that blossomed in the twentieth century. From there, many of these fabrics were brought back to Holland and other colonial countries when African immigrants moved there, carrying these fabrics with them as a reminder of home. The material, as well as Shonibare's quoting of a recognisable visual form of European art, is indicative of the hybridity of influences many modern migrants and their families experience.

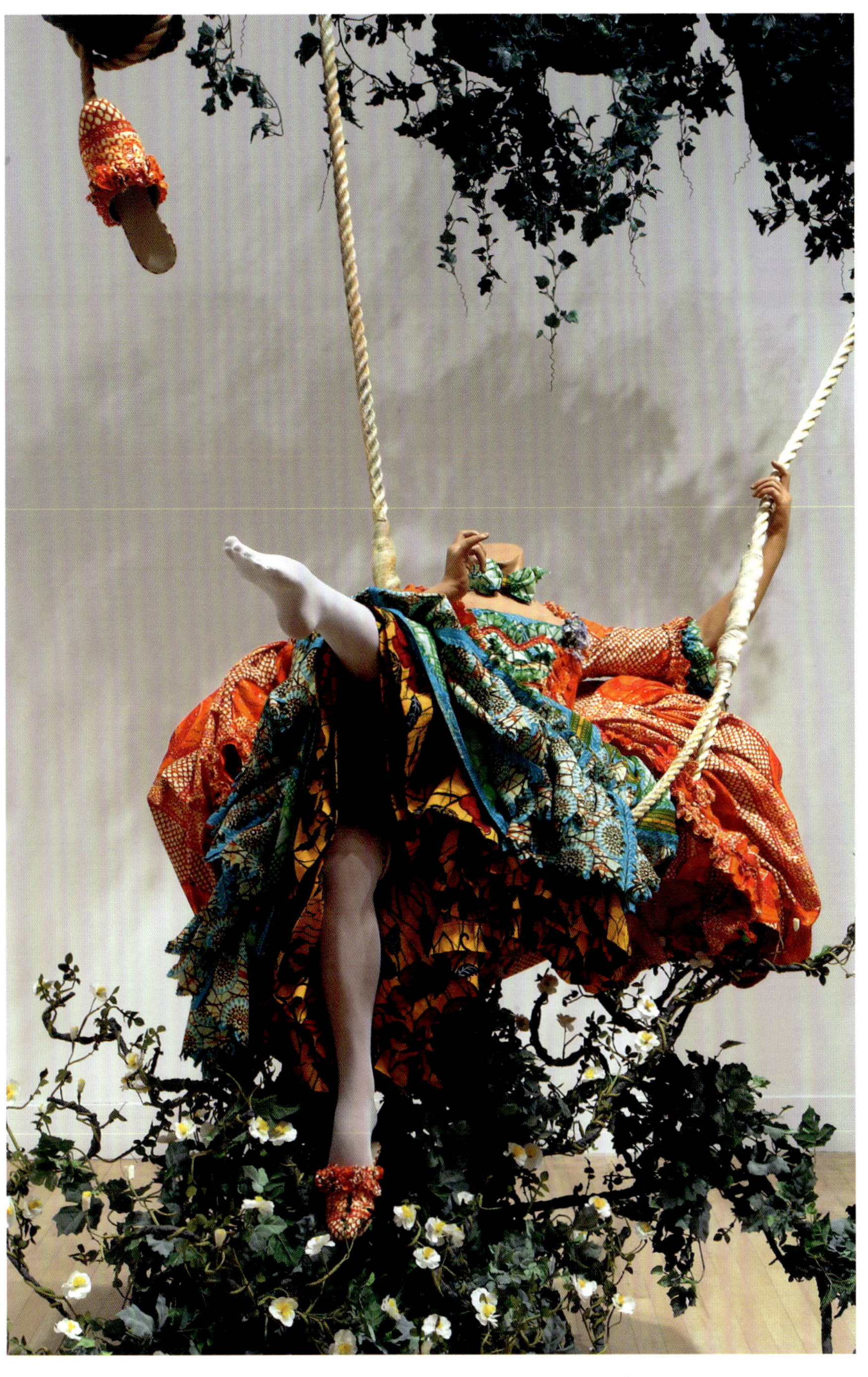

Tania Bruguera 1968–
Made in India 2001
Cotton, glass, paper and tea. Overall display dimensions variable

Cuban-born performance and installation artist Tania Bruguera made this work during a residency she undertook at the Khoj International Artists' Association in New Delhi, India. The work consists of a panel of dyed red cotton as well as undyed lighter panels on each side. Used teabags flank the red fabric piece, adorning it in an overlapping pattern that resembles metal armour or jewellery. Bruguera wanted to create a work that examined themes of deculturation, particularly honing in on the way the British exported Indian tea to Britain before repackaging it and re-importing it to India at a higher price and as a symbol of Britishness.

The rough and undyed cotton fabric may also be seen as part of Bruguera's examination of Indian trade with the British. It is a nod to calico, a key textile the British East India Company exported from India at great profit to themselves and, consequently, the British Empire generally. (The name 'calico' itself derives from Calicut, the English colonial name for the Southern Indian city of Kozhikode.) Due to the more favourable growing conditions in India and the cheaper labour that arose as a result of colonisation, seventeenth-century British traders were able to sell cotton fabrics at prices that undercut those produced in Britain's cotton capital, Norwich. In order to protect British interests, Parliament passed a law banning the importing of dyed fabrics, leading importers to concentrate their efforts on rougher, undyed Indian calico throughout the eighteenth and nineteenth centuries.

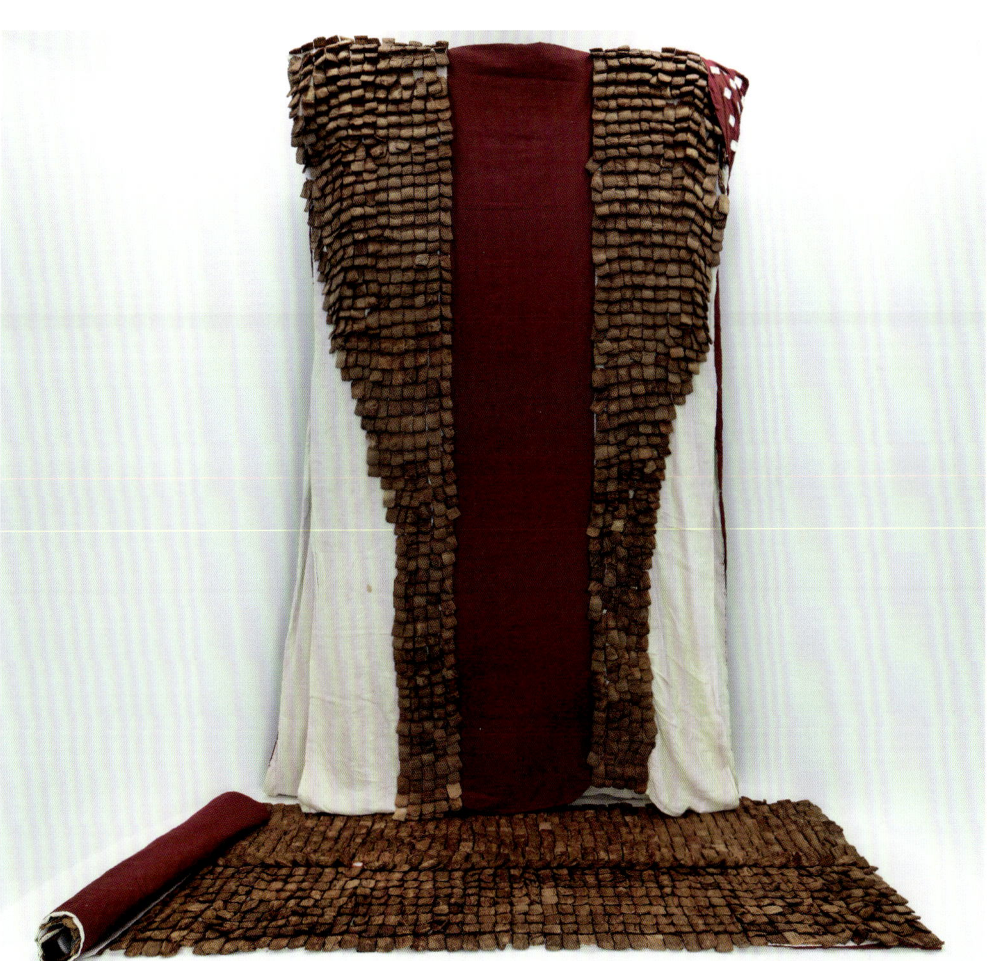

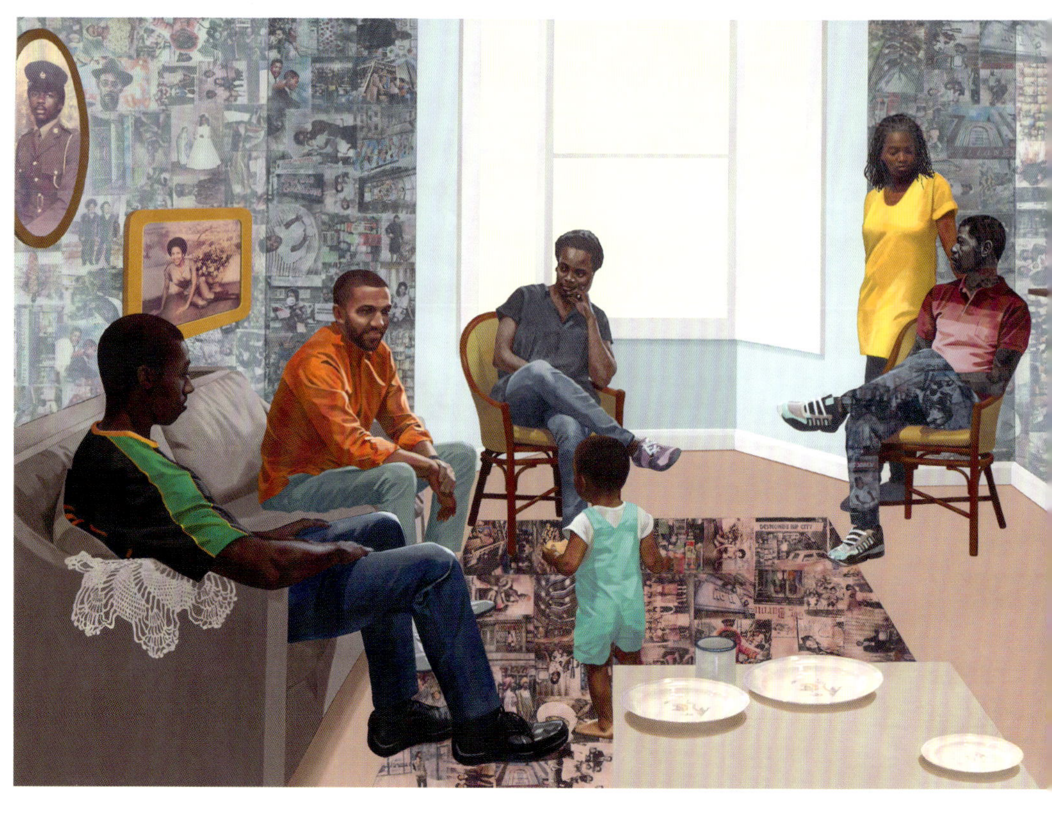

Njideka Akunyili Crosby 1983–
Remain, Thriving 2018
Acrylic paint, transfer print on paper, coloured pencil and pastel on paper 192.5 × 364.8

Sitting around in a wallpapered front room, an imagined group of grandchildren of members of the so-called Windrush Generation (a generation of post-war Commonwealth British citizens who moved to Britain from Caribbean countries) sit around speaking. On the news, a segment covering the scandalous detention and deportation of members of this generation is playing. Upon closer inspection, the wallpaper and carpet are made of a composite of images, which Akunyili Crosby chose from the Black Cultural Archives in Brixton.

A culturally important space, the brightly patterned front room was a central gathering place for cross-generational gatherings of Caribbean families living in Britain in the second half of the twentieth century. Though this room is slightly more streamlined aesthetically, a few recognisable vestiges of a traditional front room remain, such as a wooden radiogram. A crocheted antimacassar, another such object, is draped over the arm of the sofa. Originally a Victorian furnishing trend, antimacassars gained prominence as a response to the fashion for men oiling their hair with Macassar, an oil purportedly made with ingredients from the eponymous Dutch East Indies port. Coverings for the backs and sides of chairs, to prevent the Macassar-oiled man from damaging furnishings, became popular and were named accordingly. In many Caribbean countries, Christian missionaries placed an importance on teaching crocheting, antimacassars being an accessible and relevant application for the skill. Many members of the Windrush Generation subsequently brought a strong belief in the necessity of crocheted antimacassars with them upon their move to Britain. By the time they arrived, the fashion for the item had long passed, and their use became a symbol of Caribbean identity still recognisable to many today.

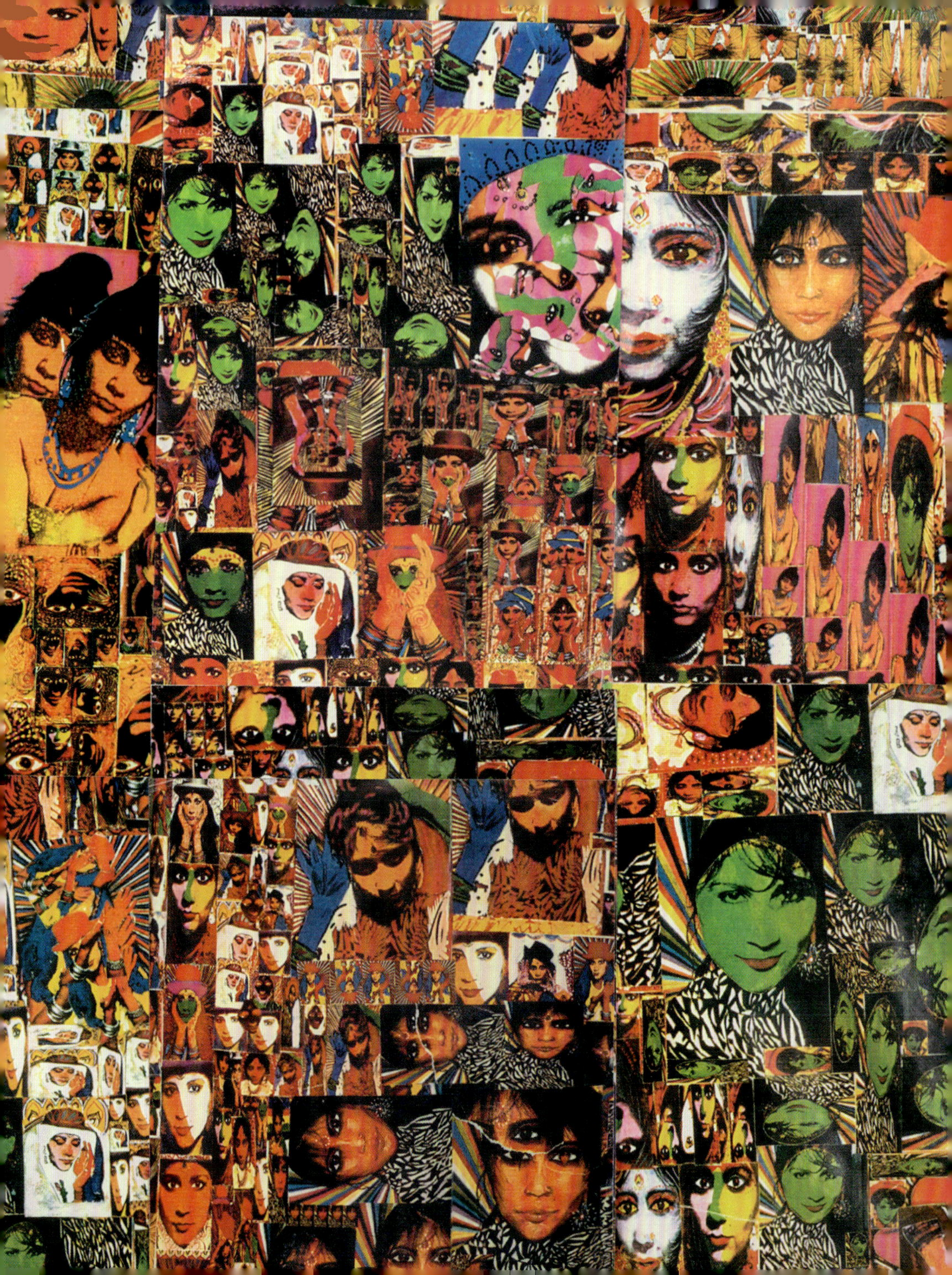

In Vogue

‘Really and truly, such amazing things are going to happen to you that you would never believe them, unless you saw them in *Vogue*.’
— Editor’s Introduction, First Edition of British *Vogue*, 1916

Founded in New York in 1892 and revamped into the avant-garde epicentre of fashion news and trend reporting by the inimitable publishing icon Condé Nast, *Vogue* is still, today, synonymous with high fashion. With its name derived from the French word for fashion, the magazine reports on fashion trends as well as other topical content, the scope of which has typically shifted slightly under its range of reigning editors. Since its establishment, *Vogue* has always pioneered the most up-to-date means of reproducible imagemaking. It included its first photograph as a story illustration before the turn of the century, in 1893, and has continued to provide space for unique and up-to-the-minute styles ever since. In this way, the history of *Vogue* is somewhat intertwined with the history of photography – art photography, fashion photography and even photojournalism.

Some of the world’s most important photographers launched their careers via the support of *Vogue*, including Edward Steichen, whose 1932 cover of British *Vogue* was the magazine’s first reproduced colour photograph. Cecil Beaton shot to fame after photographing the Sitwell family for British *Vogue* in 1926. Lee Miller appeared both in front of and behind the lens for various international editions of the magazine, ultimately publishing some of her most powerful images of the Allied Forces’ liberation of the concentration camps Dachau and Buchenwald in 1945 in American and British *Vogue*. Today, names like Annie Leibovitz and Mario Testino enjoy a similar relationship with the publication.

Through its very circulation, *Vogue* brought photographic collage to a much wider audience and provided inspiration, along with other illustrated print publications, to creatives wishing to replicate, utilise or manipulate the printed style of the magazine’s

Page 36: Chila Kumari Singh Burman *TALL FLY GIRL! Auto-Portrait* 1993 (detail, see p.59)

pages. After the Second World War, there was a mushrooming of publications that included illustrations to their stories, taking *Vogue* – either implicitly or explicitly – as their aesthetic starting point. Many artists in the 1960s also followed suit, most famously Jann Haworth and Peter Blake, in their front cover for The Beatles' *Sgt. Pepper's Lonely Hearts Club Band* album of 1967. Four years earlier, Robyn Denny created a mural for the shoe section of the menswear department store Austin Reed, in front of which the Beatles posed for their 1963 London photoshoot.

This section looks at works influenced by aspects of the culture *Vogue* created and perpetuated, from the fashion culture and cycles it reported on, to the style of posing made popular by its models, and the collaged aesthetic of print culture it helped bring about.

Berthe Morisot 1841–95
Girl on a Divan c.1885
Oil paint on canvas 61 × 50.2

In Morisot's painting, a girl leans backwards against a divan, a low couch-like form of seating with a back and sides, designed for multiple people. Typically found in Ottoman countries, the divan became fashionable in France and much of Europe during the nineteenth-century craze for 'Orientalism', when displaying such a piece of furniture in one's European home was a mark of one's worldliness and sophistication. For the impressionists, painting the modernity of their world also meant documenting its latest fashion trends meticulously. The sitter's outfit is thoroughly on trend for the 1880s, when women's clothing was suddenly drowned with ornamentation, including ribbons, frills and ruffles like those which adorn the neckline of the sitter's dress. Her hair, too, follows the vogue for tight, clean hair away from the face, no stray escaping ringlet in sight.

Throughout the late 1870s and 1880s, one silhouette dominated women's dress shapes – the princess line. In most dresses, a horizontal seam brings together the skirt and the bodice of the dress; the princess line style did away with this element entirely. Instead, all seams were entirely vertical, creating a slim waist and longer-silhouetted body. It also meant, however, that women could not sit at a ninety-degree angle due to the restrictions of the vertical shape. The combination of the fashion for lower-sitting furniture and the princess line was not a particularly comfortable one for women, and while a modern viewer may mistake the sitter's pose as one of relaxed repose, she is, in fact, sitting as upright as possible in this restrictive style – which may explain her tight expression.

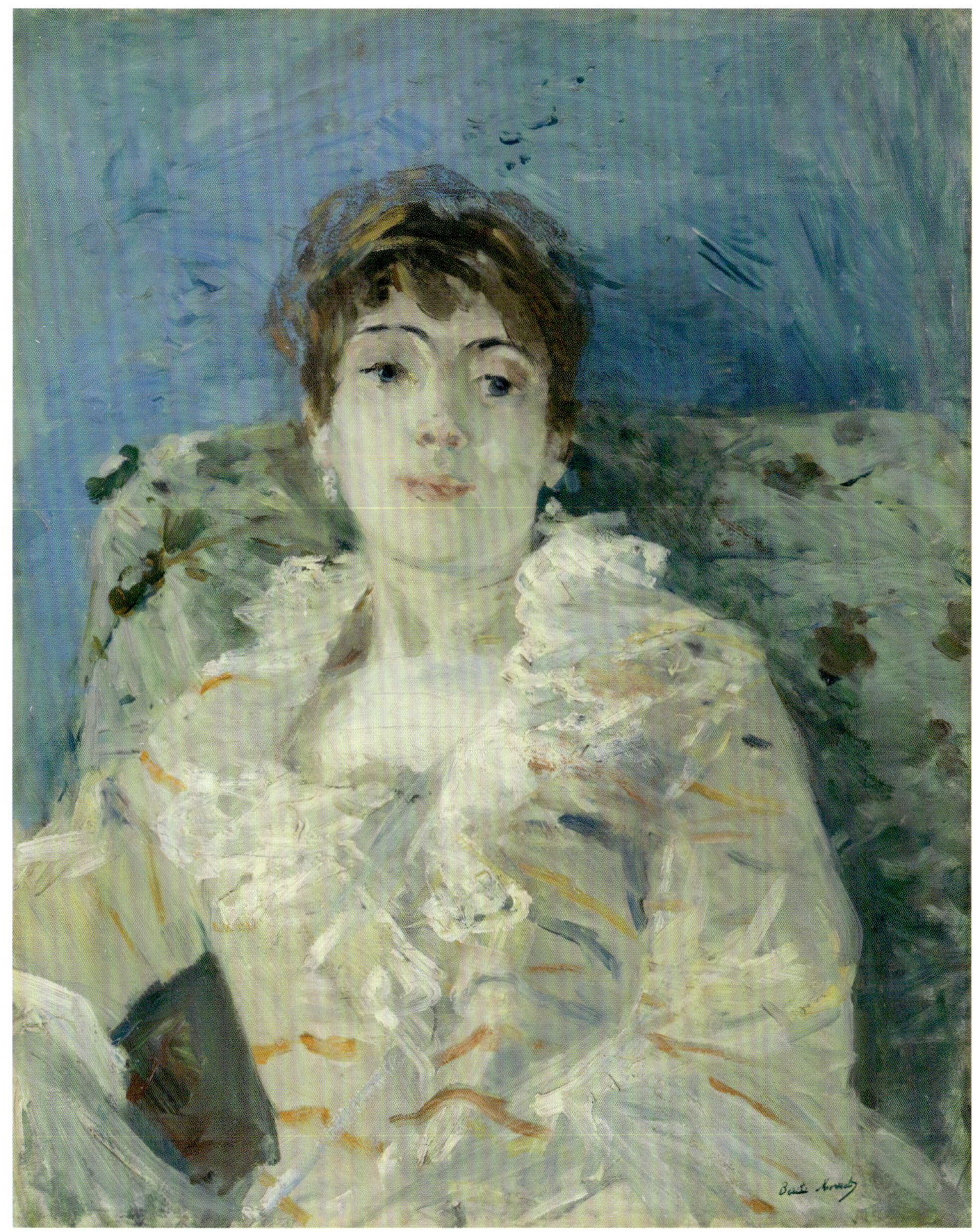

Florine Stettheimer 1871–1944
Spring Sale at Bendel's 1921
Oil paint on canvas 127 × 101.6

Plush red carpeting and curtains frame a frenetic scene of women, maids and shop assistants interacting with one another. Draped in an array of fabric rolls and items of clothing, the women rush around, diving and wrestling items from out of each other's hands and even, in one case, off one another's bodies. Standing calmly to one side of the chaos, a man – presumably the store's eponymous owner, Henri Willis Bendel – surveys the scene.

Though Bendel initially established his New York City shop as a millinery, he soon expanded into clothing, and, by the time this painting was created in 1921, Bendel's occupied a grand eight-storey building on West 57th Street, near the city's best-known luxury hotel, The Plaza. Bendel was an innovative businessman and pioneered a number of retail practices that we see as common today: he was the first to import Paris couturiers (including Coco Chanel) to his American store, put on fashion shows, and introduced the idea of trying make-up on in the store before buying it. Most pertinently for Stettheimer's painting, Bendel was one of the first retailers in the United States to introduce and promote seasonal sales. For a time, Bendel's was the only major luxury retailer in New York City offering regular sales, making it the only place shoppers could go if they wished for a specific piece they couldn't afford at full price. This led to a particularly frenzied and cut-throat environment that only eased once other department stores in the city began to introduce similar events.

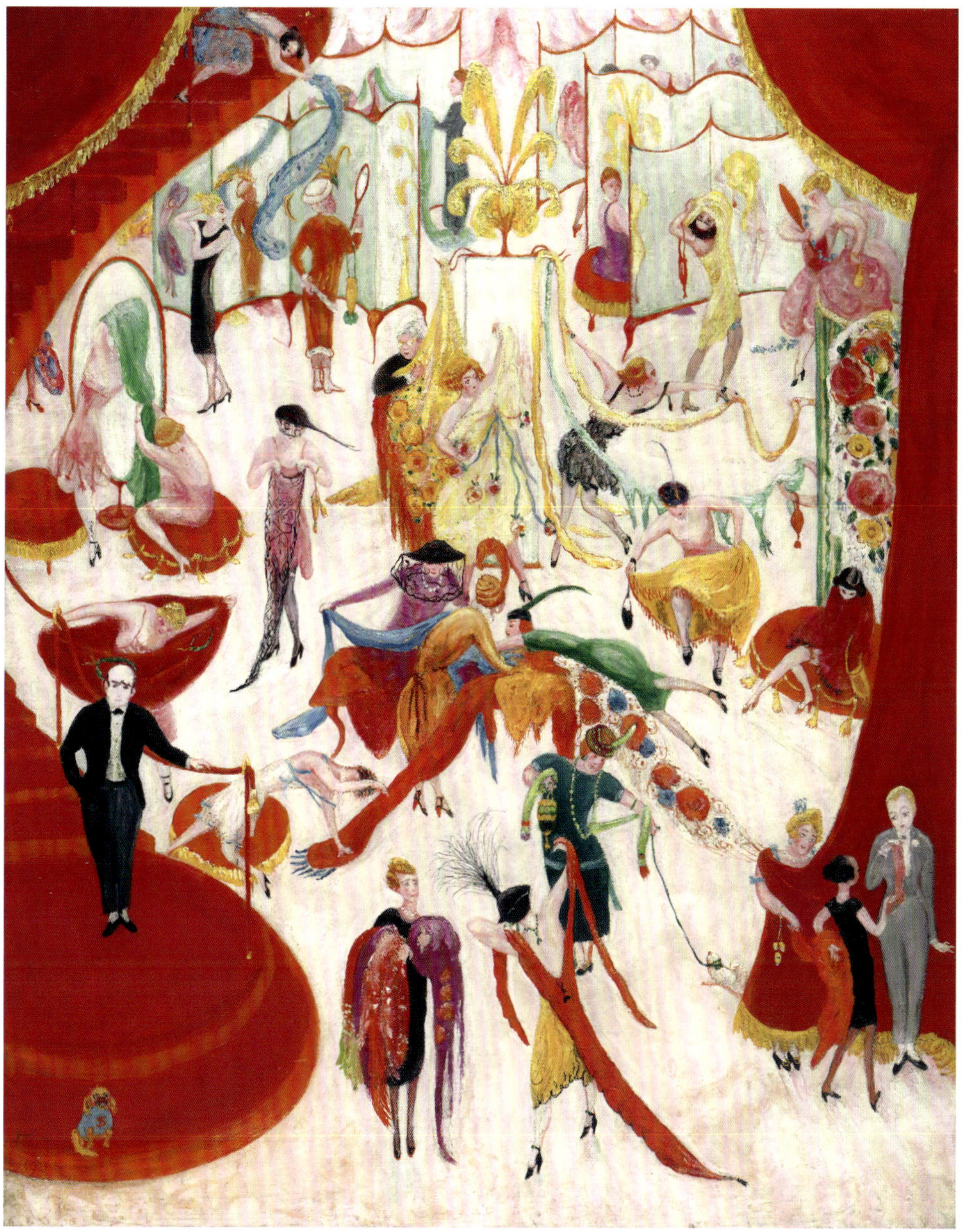

Nina Hamnett 1890–1956
A Gentleman with a Top Hat (George Manuel Unwin Esq) 1921
Oil paint on canvas 147.3 × 86.3

Hamnett's *Gentleman with a Top Hat* concentrates on a sitter dressed smartly, sitting rather formally for his portrait. Though he wears formal British day dress, suggesting a desire to be seen as somewhat traditional, the elements in the background tell another story. To the left of the sitter, a bright red patterned textile undulates over a piece of furniture, while an interesting red-and-white jug sits at his feet. In their style, colouring and pattern, both are reminiscent of the work of the Omega Workshop.

The Omega Workshop was established in 1913 by a selection of members of the Bloomsbury Group, including Vanessa Bell, Roger Fry, Duncan Grant and, pertinently, Hamnett herself. The collective aimed to break down the division between the fine arts and crafts, and to make artistic expressions of the Bloomsbury Group's work more accessible to the public while also providing a new income opportunity for members struggling to make ends meet from artwork sales alone. Many members of the Bloomsbury Group were known for their unconventional familial arrangements, often maintaining long-term non-heterosexual and/or non-monogamous romantic arrangements at a time when these were unacceptable both legally and socially. The Omega Workshops made household items, clothing and textiles, developing patterns and forms that reflected, in more literal aesthetic terms, their rethinking of domestic life and relationships. Hamnett's placement of Omega or Omega-like pieces in the background of this portrait suggests the sitter may live according to more bohemian values than his formal dress might initially suggest.

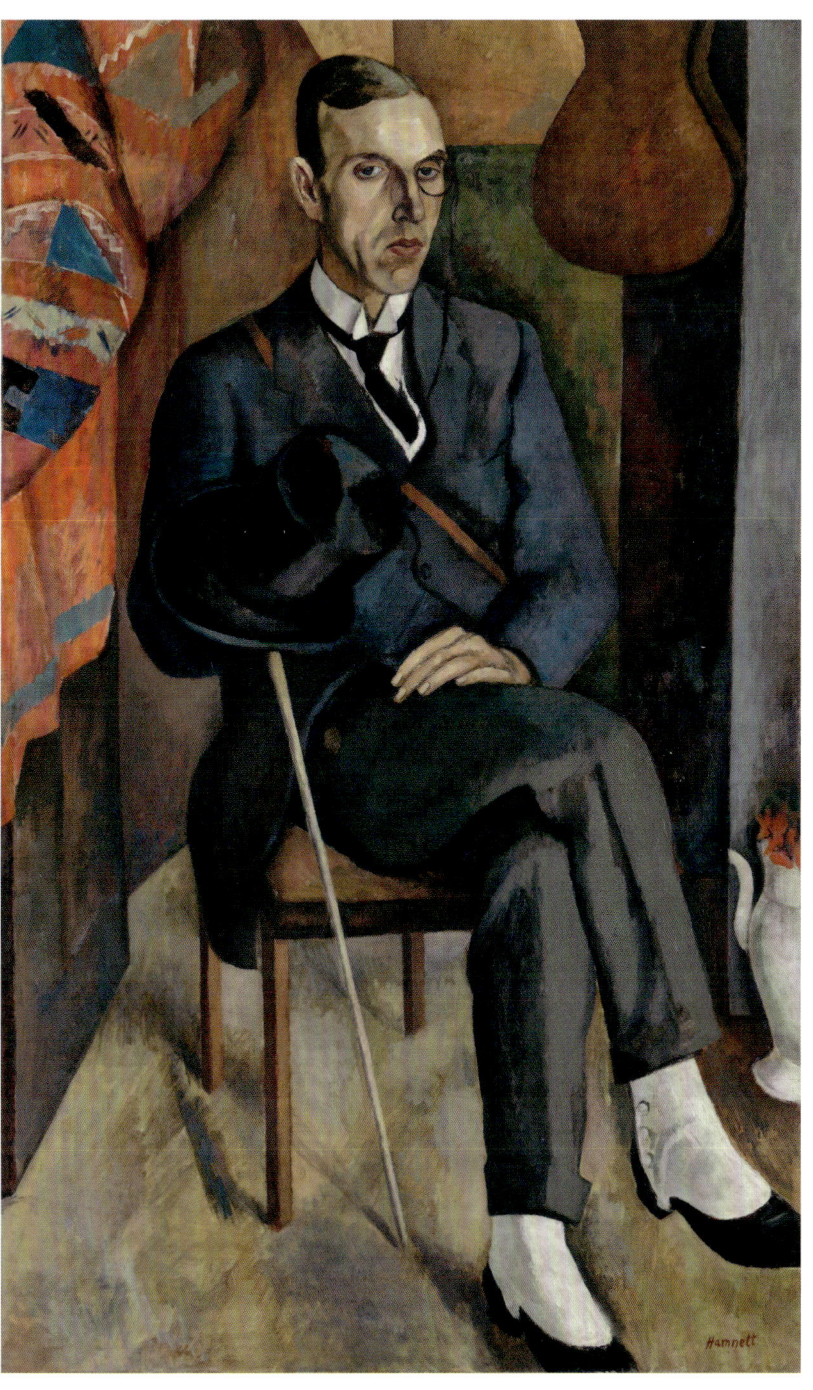
Hamnett

Piet Mondrian 1872–1944
Composition with Yellow, Blue and Red 1937–42
Oil paint on canvas 72.7 × 69.2

With his pioneering exploration of pure form and colour, Mondrian was a major contributor to the prominent Dutch avant-garde De Stijl movement as well as one of the most accomplished artists of the twentieth century. As such, when fashion designer Yves Saint Laurent wished to distinguish himself and his clothes as radically modern in his Autumn/Winter 1965 collection, he chose to reproduce Mondrian's paintings on shift dresses. The use of Mondrian's sparse and simple lines and colour blocks intensified the increasingly simplified silhouettes of miniskirts and shift dresses pioneered by Mary Quant in London and Courrèges in Paris. Though Yves Saint Laurent's dresses were slightly longer than those that were *de rigueur* in London, their simple shape still mirrored women's burgeoning desire to reflect their freer status in society by dressing in a manner that did not constrain their movement. To honour Mondrian's planes, Saint-Laurent carefully hid the seams of the jersey fabric he used in these dresses, so that he could achieve as smooth a 'canvas' as possible.

In spite of his French-sounding name, Mondrian was originally from the Netherlands, Gallicising his name to indicate his integration into the interwar Parisian avant-garde. Though he created some of his finest work in France, he did not find much commercial success there until after Saint Laurent's use of his work. Four years after the collection and twenty-seven years after his death, Mondrian's first ever French retrospective was at the Musée de l'Orangerie in Paris's Tuileries Garden.

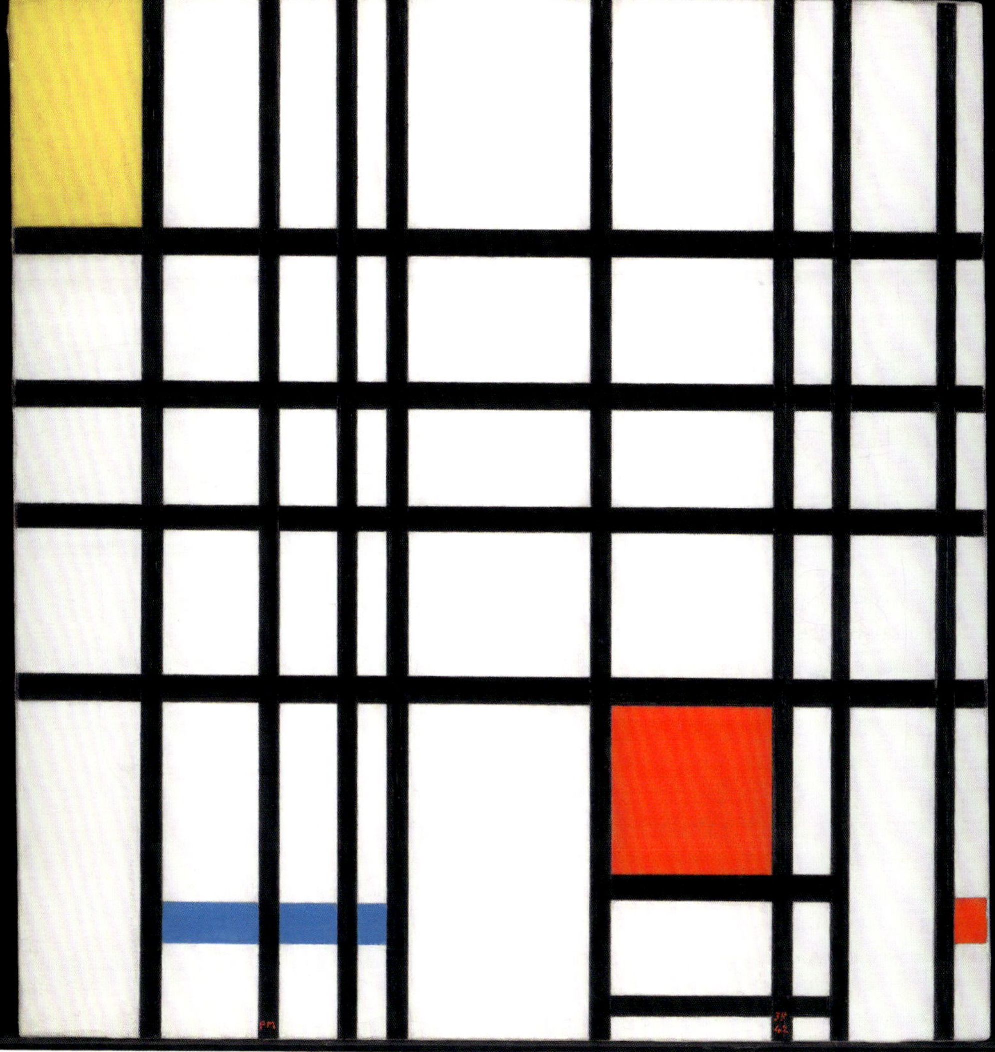

Claes Oldenburg 1929–2022
Lipsticks in Piccadilly Circus, London 1966
Printed paper on postcard on board 20.3 × 25.4

Claes Oldenburg's *Lipsticks in Piccadilly Circus* pays homage to the influence of fashion and fashion media in Britain, both aesthetically and through its subject matter. The Swedish artist created this work on a trip to the English capital, choosing the central London site of Piccadilly Circus as his backdrop. Ever since Regent Street and Oxford Street became major centres of London's retail scene in the late nineteenth and early twentieth centuries, Piccadilly Circus has served as the meeting point of the city's theatre and fashion districts. As such, it became a popular place for major companies to place billboards advertising their goods.

In the post-war period, the magazine sector expanded rapidly and, with its increasing circulation, became an alternative place to prominently advertise one's product or company. This rapid growth of advertising media – combined with a government plan to completely overhaul the area in the 1960s – led to a sense that the bright lights and hectic juxtapositions of Piccadilly Circus were not long for this world.

Oldenburg placed printed images of lipsticks, which look like they have just been cut out of a magazine, over the well-known statue of Anteros to create a physical representation of print media's potential to eclipse the current form of Piccadilly Circus and take up its mantle in the wake of urban development.

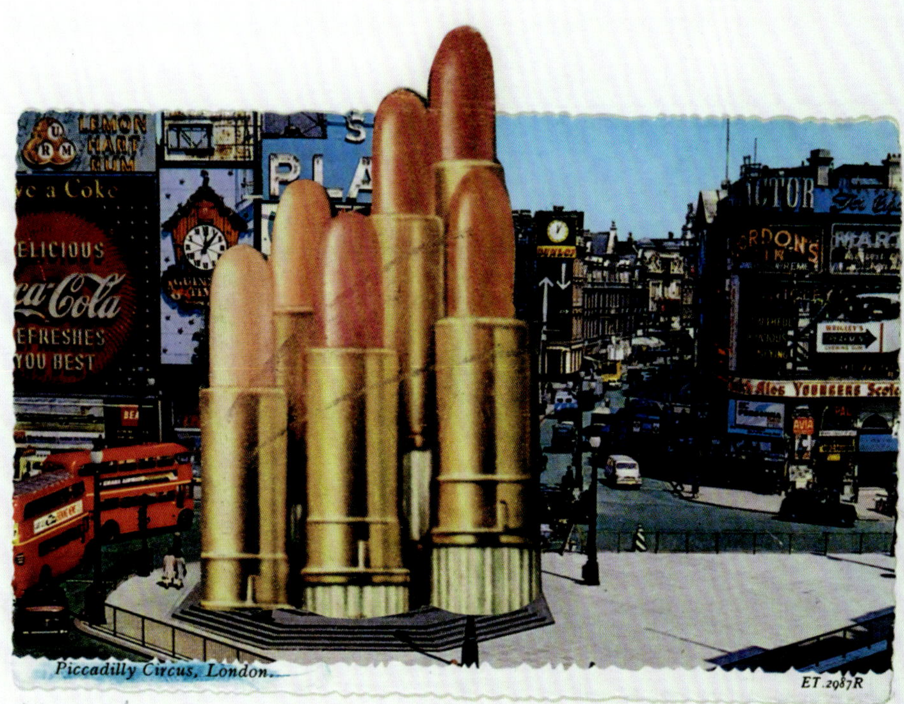
LEMON HART RUM
YOU BEST
Piccadilly Circus, London.
ET.2987R
Lipstick mon.
Oldenburg 1966.

James Barnor 1929–
Drum Cover Girl Erlin Ibreck at Trafalgar Square, London 1966
Gelatin silver print on paper 48.2 × 47.9

Ghanaian-born photographer James Barnor captured this image of fashion model Erlin Ibreck standing in Trafalgar Square when he lived in London in the 1960s as an option for the front cover of the South African publication *Drum*. Thought to have been the first lifestyle magazine specifically aimed at a Black audience in the entire African continent, *Drum* skilfully and seamlessly melded a fiercely anti-apartheid editorial position and scathing coverage of the conditions of life in South African townships with a celebration of Black lifestyle and fashion content.

In this photograph, Barnor shoots his model in a manner akin to the way in which Western fashion magazines were depicting white fashion models. British model Twiggy, for example, was photographed the very same year in the middle of a London street, standing in a similar stance and wearing a mini dress. In the wake of Yves Saint Laurent's referencing of Mondrian in his Autumn/Winter 1965 collection, it was also becoming increasingly popular for cover shoots to subtly (and not so subtly) refer back to important works of art, giving their cover story or new fashion more artistic weight. Barnor's image of Ibreck recalls the famous moment in 1936 when surrealist artist Sheila Legge, wearing a straight white dress, performed as a headless 'Phantom' in Trafalgar Square, with pigeons perching in the palms of her hands. This amalgamation of two different types of image sends a glamorous yet powerful political message to the Black readers of *Drum* magazine: that they, too, are worthy of all rights, including the right to feel beautiful and to be included as fashion models in magazine spreads and covers.

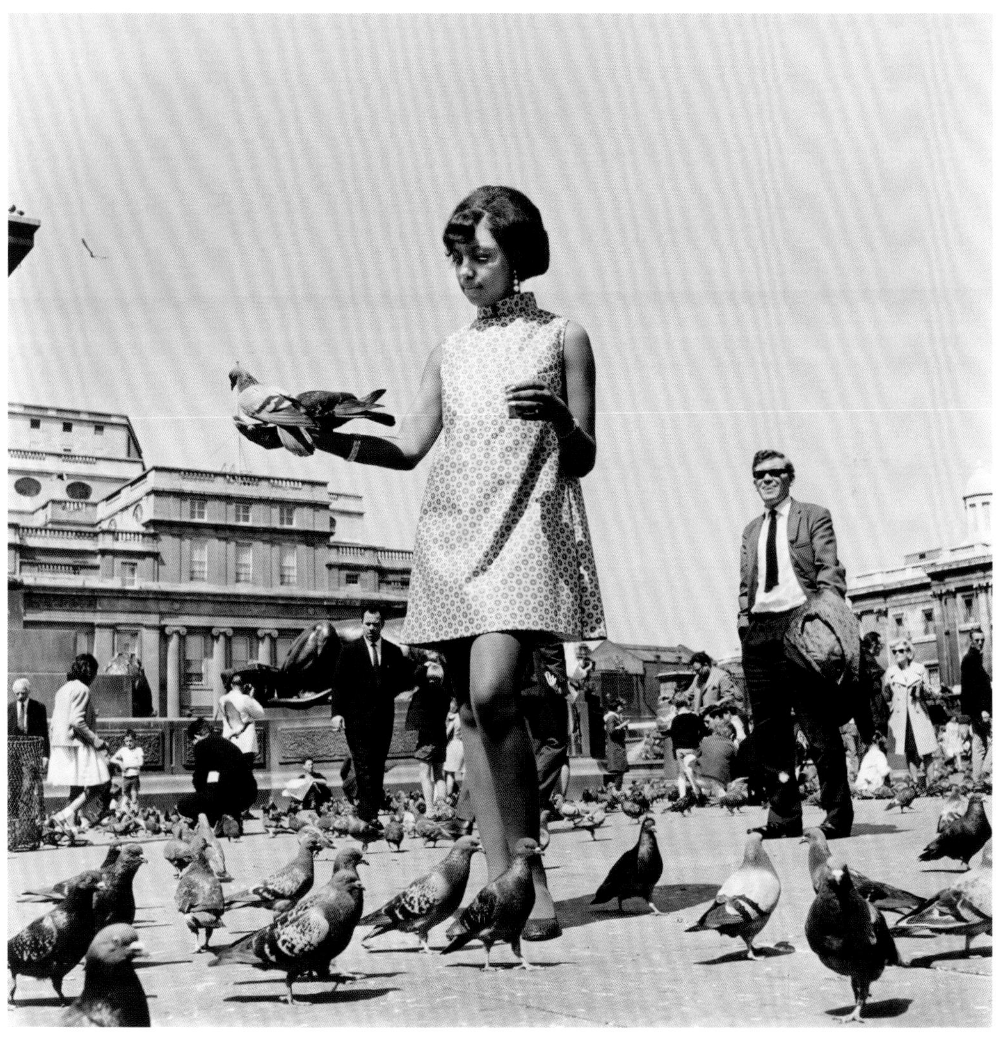

Eduardo Paolozzi 1924–2005
It's a Psychological Fact Pleasure Helps your Disposition 1948
From *Ten Collages from BUNK*
Printed papers on card 36.2 × 24.4

In the aftermath of the Second World War, most of Europe was left to reckon with the emotional and physical destruction warfare had left in its wake. Economies struggled to rebuild basic infrastructure from the rubble left behind, poverty and displacement were rampant, and rationing remained in full force. In contrast, the United States was left mostly unscathed due to its distance from the conflict and, without the sudden need to rebuild ravaged housing, roads and agricultural sites, enjoyed a relative economic boom. For many people living in Europe, America took on an air of inaccessible glamour. News and fashion magazines like American *Vogue* were some of the few ways people could experience this wealth and, in the domestic sphere, keep abreast of the latest gadgets and kitchen designs that were coming to market.

For some British artists, including Eduardo Paolozzi, the disparity between their lives and those of their American counterparts both attracted and repelled them to such an extent that they began to include this imagery and these themes in their art. Paolozzi created this work entirely by collaging elements he found in the advertising pages of American magazines promoting housework to middle-class women. Paolozzi continued to explore this theme for the next few years, continuously cutting out and collaging different magazine images, eventually presenting them all in a slide lecture at London's Institute of Contemporary Arts in 1952 titled *BUNK*.

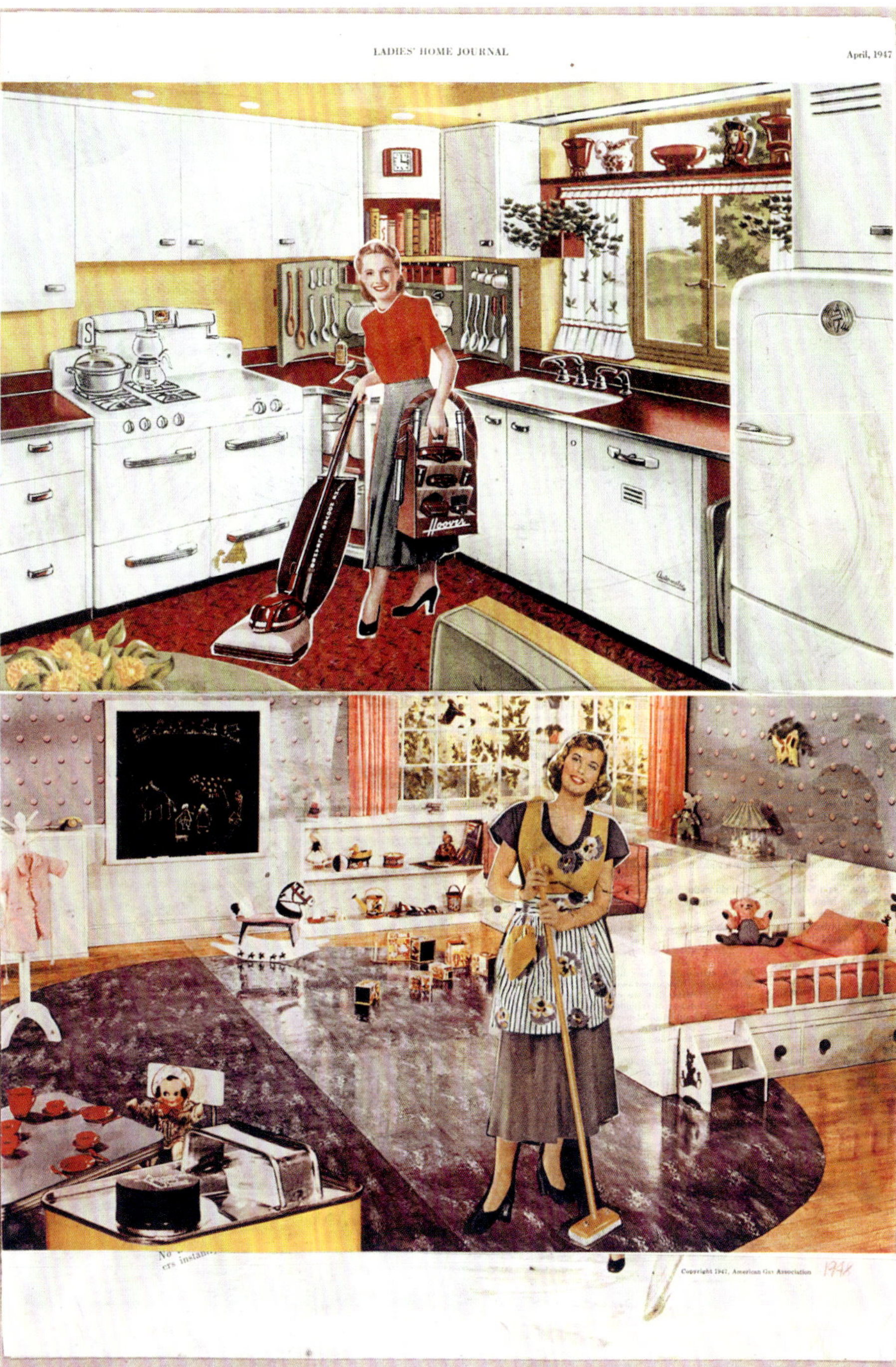
LADIES' HOME JOURNAL
April, 1947
Hoover
No
ers instan
Copyright 1947, American Gas Association

Linder 1954–
Untitled 1976
Printed papers on paper 27.9 × 19.6

Initially spurred on by the challenges of the feminist movement of the 1960s and 1970s, people began to explore the ways in which magazines written by and for women might be contributing to society's sexist pressures. For this work, made entirely of cuttings from magazines, Linder burned holes in the space where the woman's eyes had originally appeared, replacing them with cut-out eyes from elsewhere before inserting the image of the fork into them. The use of collage transforms three initially benign images into a motif that is rather violent.

For the artist herself, the use of magazine scraps became the very core of her artistic practice:

> When I began to work solely in photomontage, during the last weeks of 1976 and through into what felt like a very New Year, I used simply a surgeon's scalpel as my paintbrush and magazines became my new palette. A sheet of glass was the bed for the blade, and all the magazine cutouts were carefully stored in boxes labelled 'Mouths', 'Eyes', 'Domestic Utensils', etc.[3]

Linder amassed images from women's fashion magazines as well as from pornographic magazines, eliding them to form a commentary on the patriarchal nature of both kinds of publications and their inevitable catering to the male gaze. The focus on the eyes themselves in this work may be read as a more literal play on the notion of the gaze and the debate of whose gaze print publications serve to gratify.

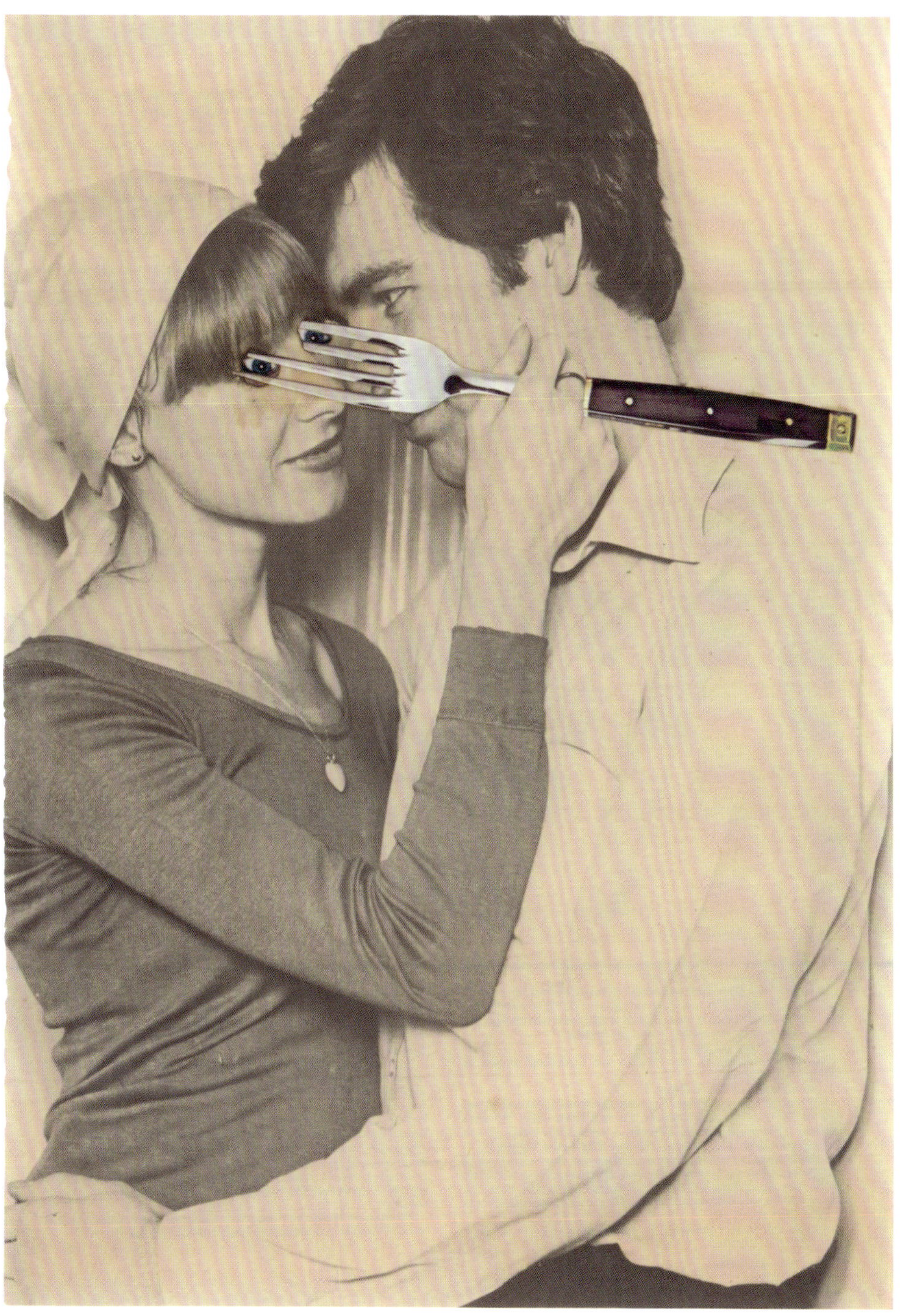

Jason Evans 1968–
[no title] 1991
From the series *Strictly*
C-print on paper 80.5 × 80.5

Evans created this image along with stylist Simon Foxton for *i-D* magazine, one of a number of 1990s magazines that began to merge high art, fashion and commercial photographic practice to a greater extent than ever before. This work is part of a series called *Strictly*, which consists of similarly formatted images. Each features a young Black man standing outdoors in an unremarkable though identifiably British suburban locale. In each shot, the model wears clothing that fuses streetwear trends with the traditional dress of the British upper classes. In this particular work, the model wears a suit and Derby shoes, but the trousers are cropped and rolled up as if they were shorts.

As their name suggests, Derby shoes emerged in nineteenth-century Britain as a shoe to wear while hunting in the countryside. Gradually, people began to wear them merely to attend Derby Days, to indicate their general participation in the sport at other times. Gradually, they became an acceptable shoe to wear around town, too, not just while engaging in rural sporting activities. This trajectory is not dissimilar to the one sportswear was enjoying in Britain and the United States in 1991. Basketball shorts, for example, were cut in a baggy loose manner to encourage freedom of movement and to allow for air to circulate and efficiently cool down sweaty players. Due to their comfort, many people who were not athletes began to incorporate shorts into their wardrobe, styling them in interesting and experimental ways. Though the clothing and replicated conditions in each work clearly expose this as a professional series, the individual photographs are shot to emulate street fashion, slyly suggesting that these were merely snapshots of men the photographer encountered by happy accident.

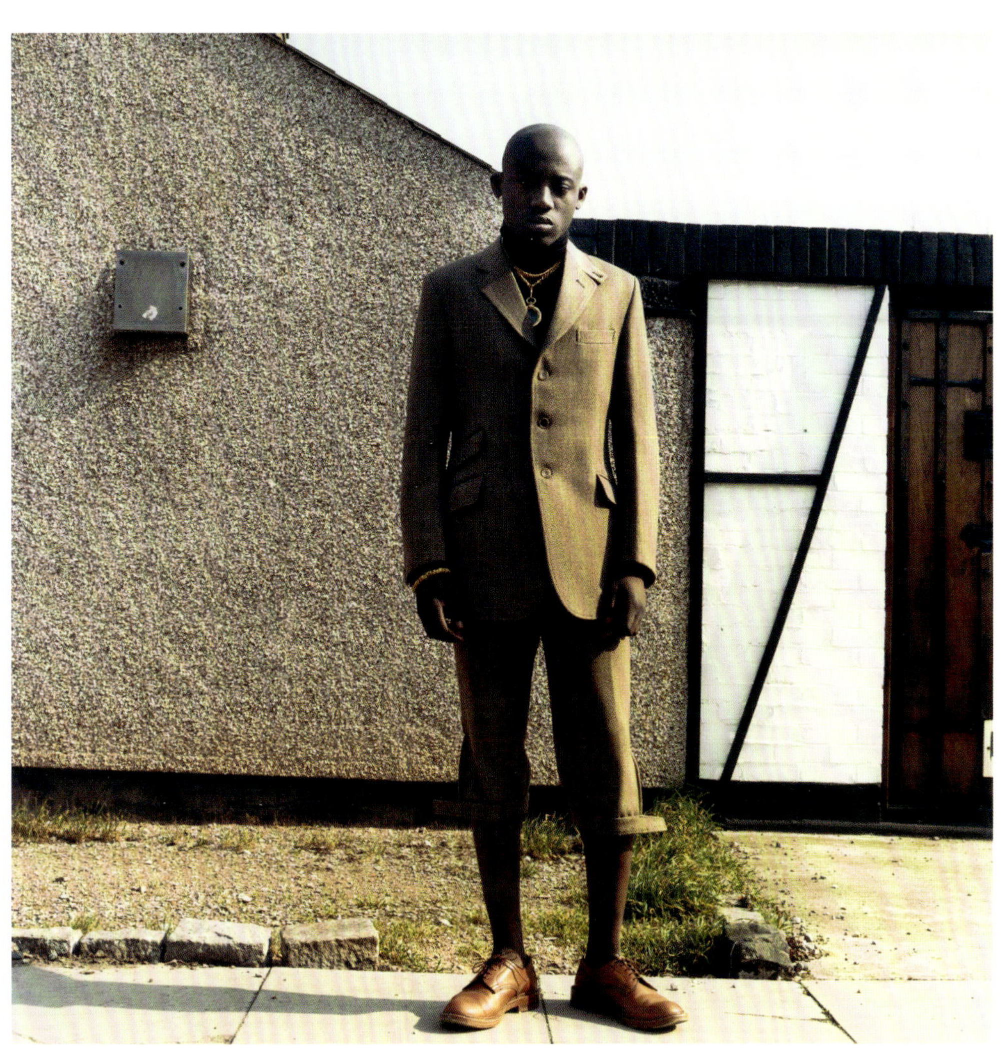

Chila Kumari Singh Burman 1957–
TALL FLY GIRL! Auto-Portrait (Fly Girl series) 1993
Digital prints on paper, on paper and board 235.5 × 115.5 × 2.5

In *TALL FLY GIRL! Auto-Portrait (Fly Girl series)*, Burman collaged together hundreds of copies of what she calls her auto-portraits. Burman posed for a set of black-and-white images of herself, hand painted each image and placed them in a grid-like formation before further manipulating their style and finish using a laser photocopier. In the range of self-portraits she created, Burman modelled herself on a range of prominent female images she felt had some bearing on her life, including the goddess Kali and 1960s *Vogue* models.

The cultivated mix of manipulated self-portraiture referencing Western fashion as well as Indian influences creates a powerful statement. By inserting images of herself into a historical *Vogue*-like aesthetic, Burman reimagines a vintage *Vogue* that does not exclusively feature and celebrate white women. Her work challenges *Vogue*'s perpetuation of a racist and discriminatory concept of feminine beauty, in which Burman cannot see herself. The very form of the work's structure – a collage – is one that was only made fully possible by the rise of print magazines. This aesthetic means that even the images of Burman that do not themselves explicitly mimic 1960s *Vogue* models are read as if they are cut-outs from just such a publication, furthering the challenge to the magazine's monopoly on deciding the parameters of female beauty.

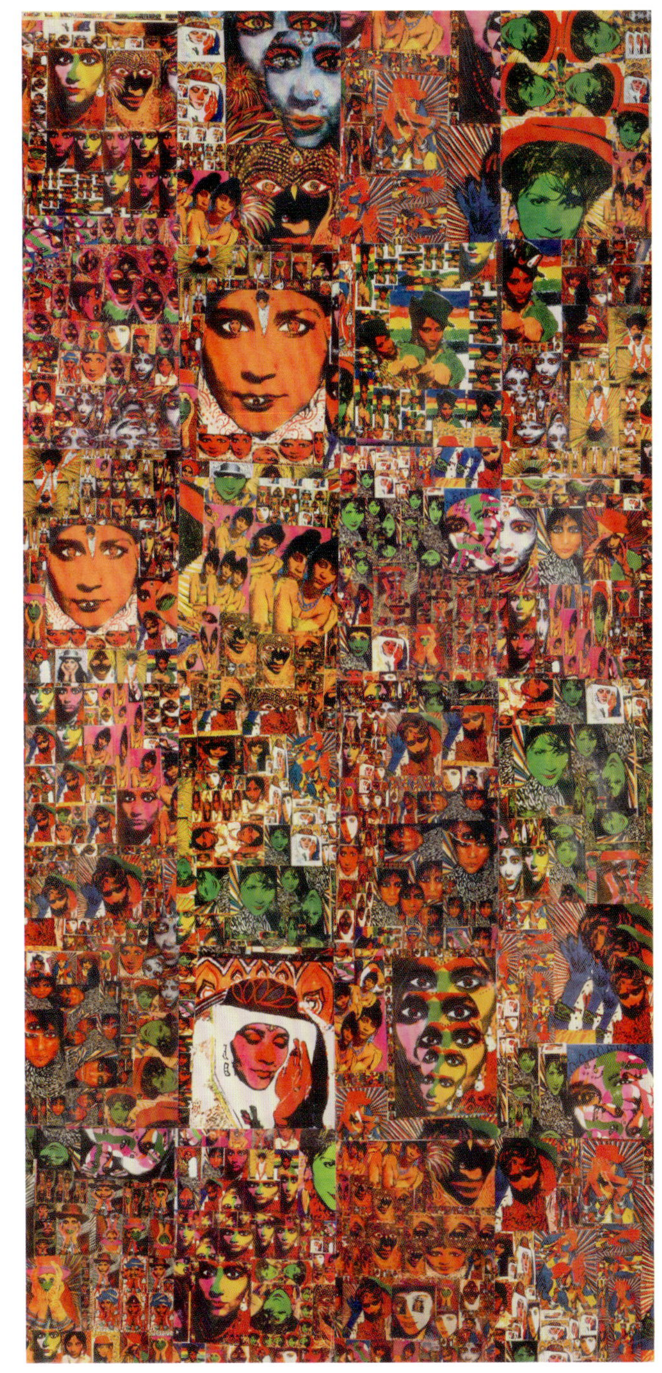

Amy Sherald 1973–
Michelle LaVaughn Robinson Obama 2018
Oil paint on canvas 183.1 × 152.6 × 7

This painting was commissioned as the official portrait to memorialise Michelle Obama's time as the First Lady of the United States of America, which ended in 2017 when her husband's second presidential term concluded. Amy Sherald intentionally created a composition that places significant emphasis on the dress Obama chose to wear. During her time as First Lady, Obama was known for her championing of young American designers such as Prabal Gurung, Zac Posen and Derek Lam, while also mixing such high-end pieces with the non-designer label J.Crew.

As the first African American First Lady of a country with a prominent history of slavery and racial discrimination, Obama's status as a glamorous figurehead was particularly revolutionary and her choice of clothing often the subject of much scrutiny. The dress she wore for this portrait was from designer Michelle Smith's Milly label, a customised version of a dress Smith produced as part of her 2017 collection. For Sherald, the patterns on the dress contained a significant symbolism: they emulate abstract works by the artist Piet Mondrian, famously placed on a set of dresses by Yves Saint Laurent in the 1960s (see pp.46–7). They also resemble the famous patterned geometric quilts made by African American women in the Alabama town of Gee's Bend since the nineteenth century. The dress merges this important folk textile tradition with more traditional Western fashion glamour, a visual echo of the blending of influences that many felt characterised Obama's time as First Lady.

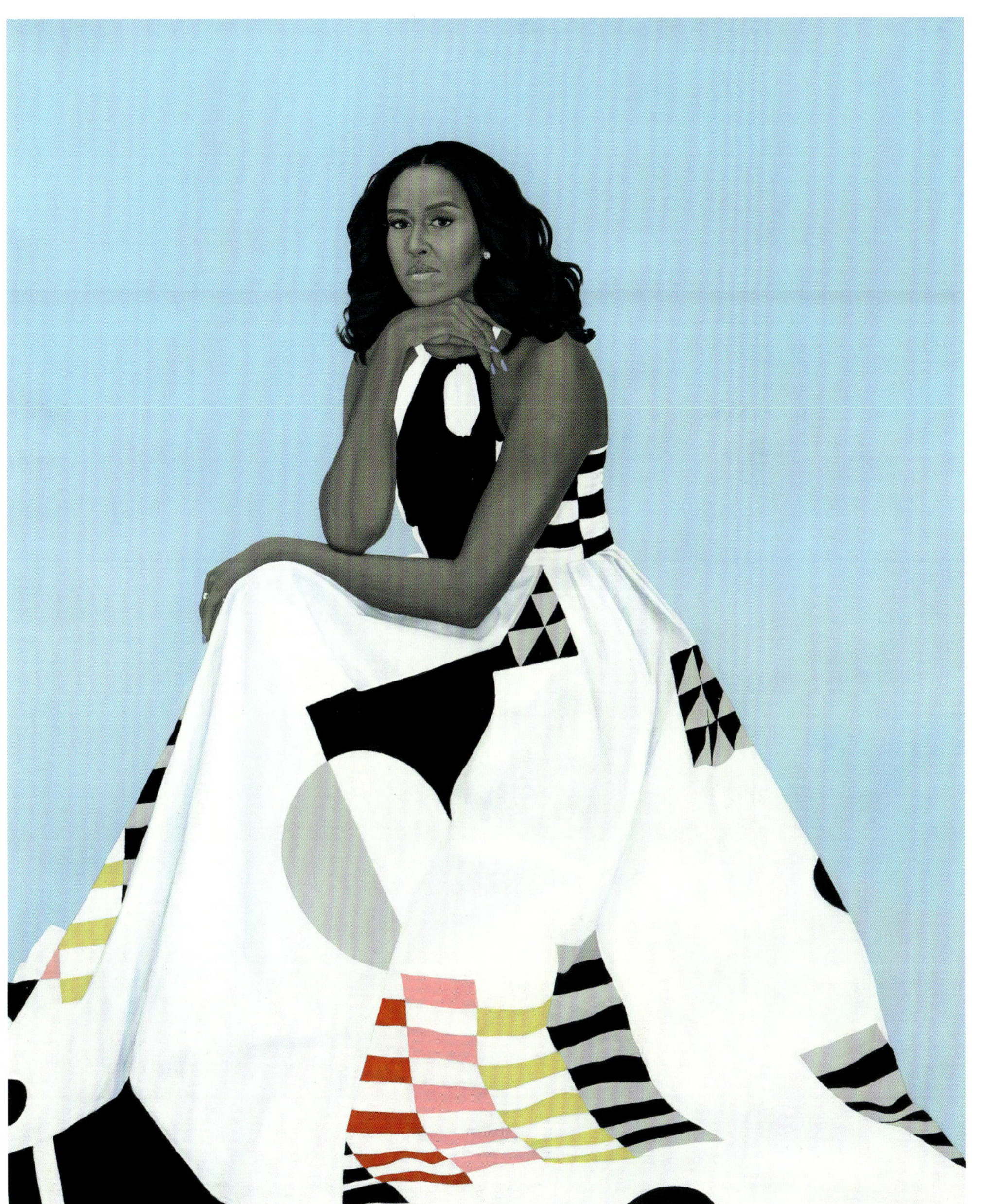

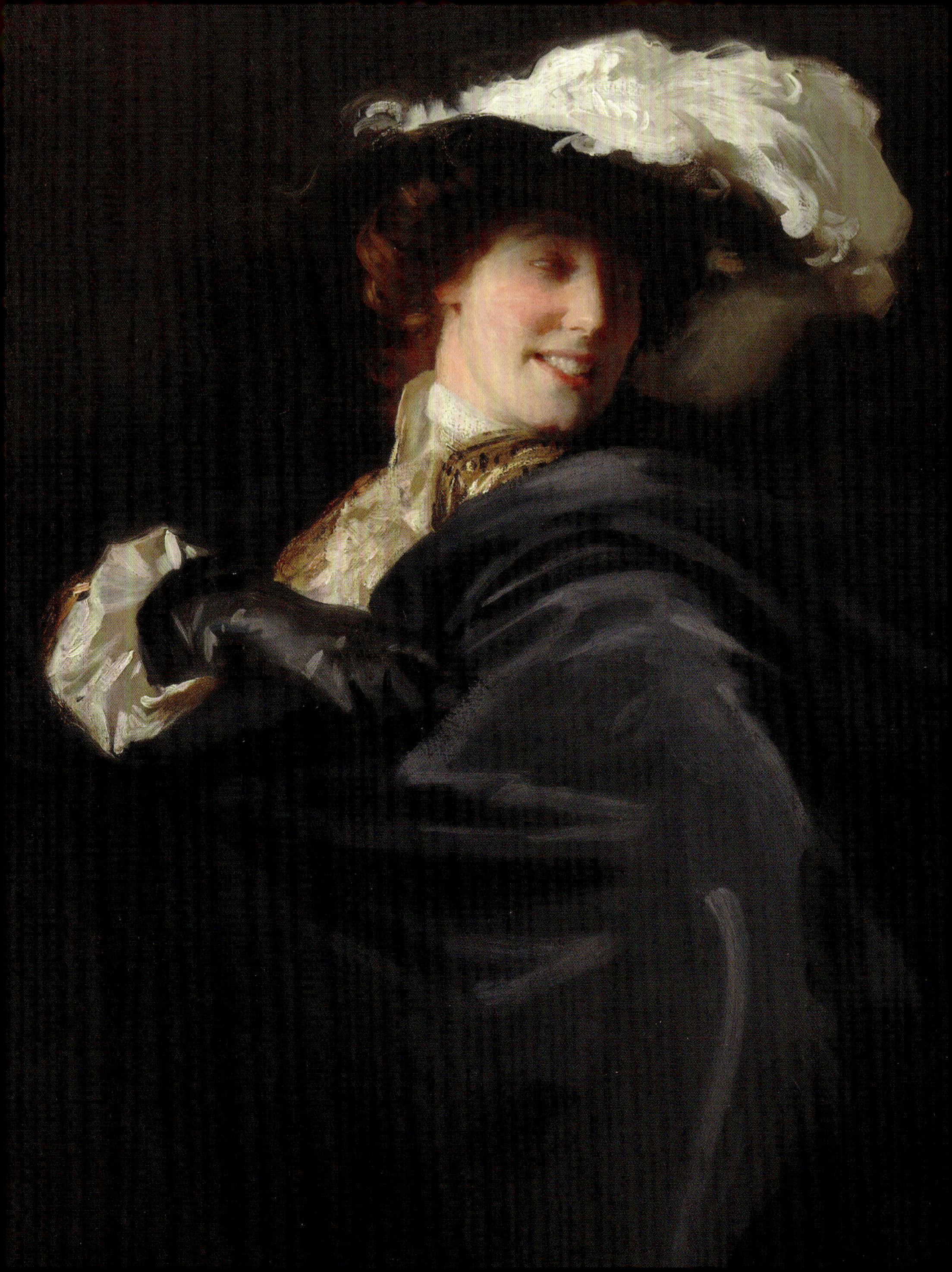

Uniform Style

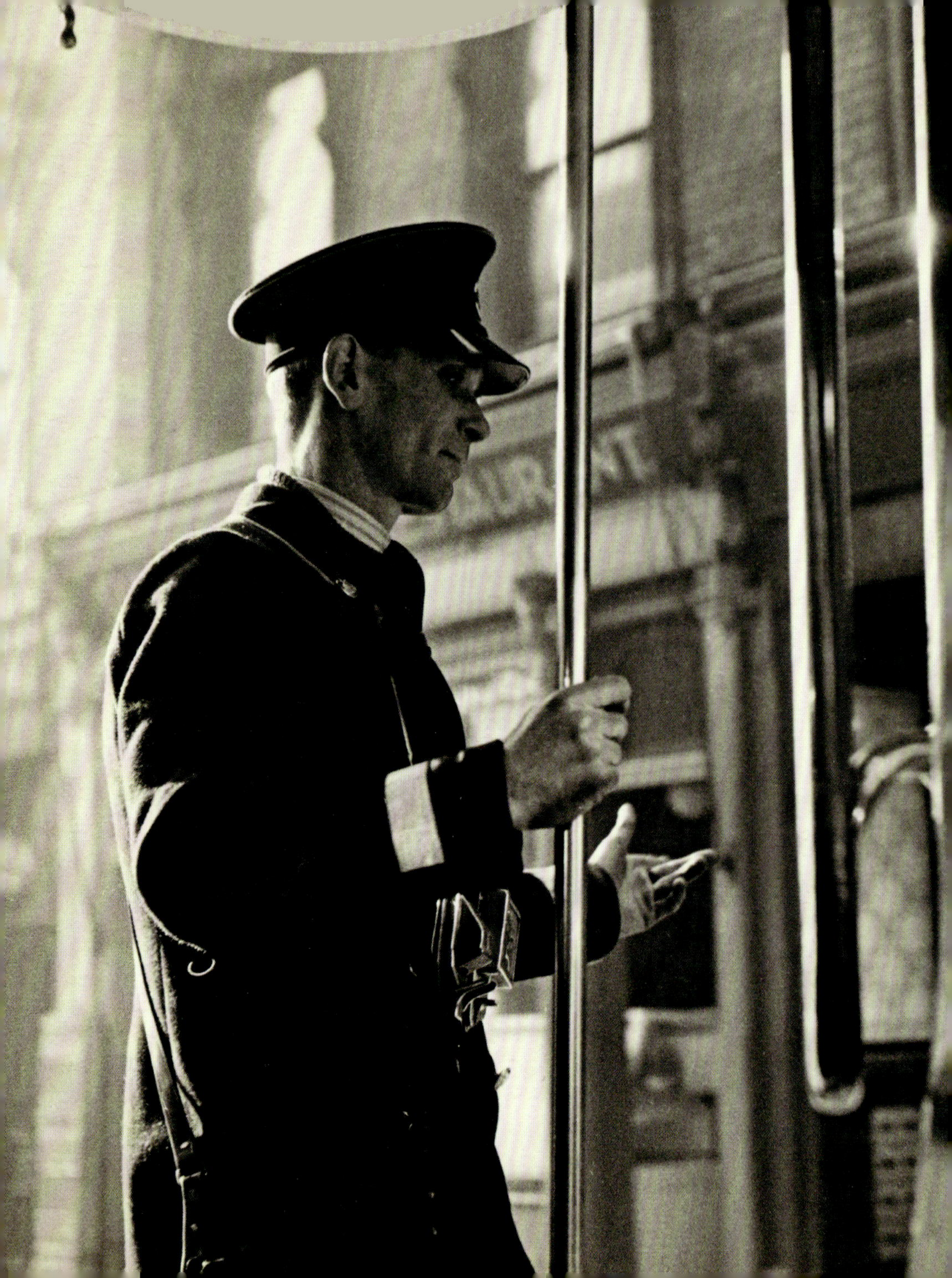

Uniforms are signifiers of identity and culture in the most explicit manner available to clothing, often denoting class, stature, achievements and, in some darker moments of history, race. During the Second World War, Jews were forced to wear yellow stars on their clothing whenever they appeared in public in order to make their identity explicit to all who laid eyes upon them. This also helped to enforce the restrictions Jews were under, ensuring they did not attempt to attend public educational institutions, or set foot in a shop or on a street from which they were banned.

Across the world, children have been wearing distinct uniforms in order to attend school for hundreds of years. In many religions, those who have dedicated their lives to the service of the religion or its institutions wear a uniform in order to denote their capacity. In some instances, various embellishments or lack thereof indicate precise status in the hierarchies of the religious order. In Roman times, only the Emperor was permitted to wear purple clothing, a practice which Elizabeth I of England loosely replicated during her own lengthy reign, when only those close to the monarch were permitted to wear the colour.

In some ways, fashion itself can be seen as a sort of uniform, a means of voluntarily identifying oneself as belonging to one specific fashion tribe or another. The pages that follow, however, stick to depictions of the more traditional, recognisable types of uniforms and dress codes, which have featured in some of the world's most interesting, beautiful and poignant works of art in the last 150 years, delving deeper into their significance and history.

Edith Tudor-Hart *London Bus Conductor* c.1930 (detail, see p.79). • Page 62: John Singer Sargent *Portrait of Ena Wertheimer: A Vele Gonfie* 1904 (detail, see p.71)

Ozias Humphry 1742–1810
Christiaan von Molhoop c.1795
Pastel on paper 72.5 × 61

This pastel portrait of an elaborately dressed Black man shows Christiaan von Molhoop, an eighteenth-century servant of Baron Nagell, who was Dutch ambassador to England during the time Humphry made this work. Nagell was known for dressing his servants in rather flamboyant and grand uniforms, with tricolour liveries that reflected the colours of the Dutch flag, and turbans and feathers that patriotically pointed to the Netherlands's extensive colonial presence in the East.

In spite of the fact that von Molhoop is wearing a servant's livery with many of the customary elements of a Dutch livery (albeit slightly embellished), his identity as a servant was lost over time. By 1909, the work was owned by London collector Sir Cuthbert Quilter. The catalogue of his collection lists the work as 'An African Prince', and when the auction house Christie's sold the painting on Sir Cuthbert's behalf in 1909, this was the title under which they advertised and auctioned it off to its new owner.

The misidentification serves as an interesting example of the importance of contextualising the clothing worn in historical paintings. Lacking the ability to identify the livery of an eighteenth-century running footman, as worn by von Molhoop, early twentieth-century connoisseurs believed the sitter to be elaborately dressed and, given his race, assumed he must be a member of African royalty, whose visit was marked by Humphry in pastel form. His true identity was only rediscovered by Tate curators in the twenty-first century.

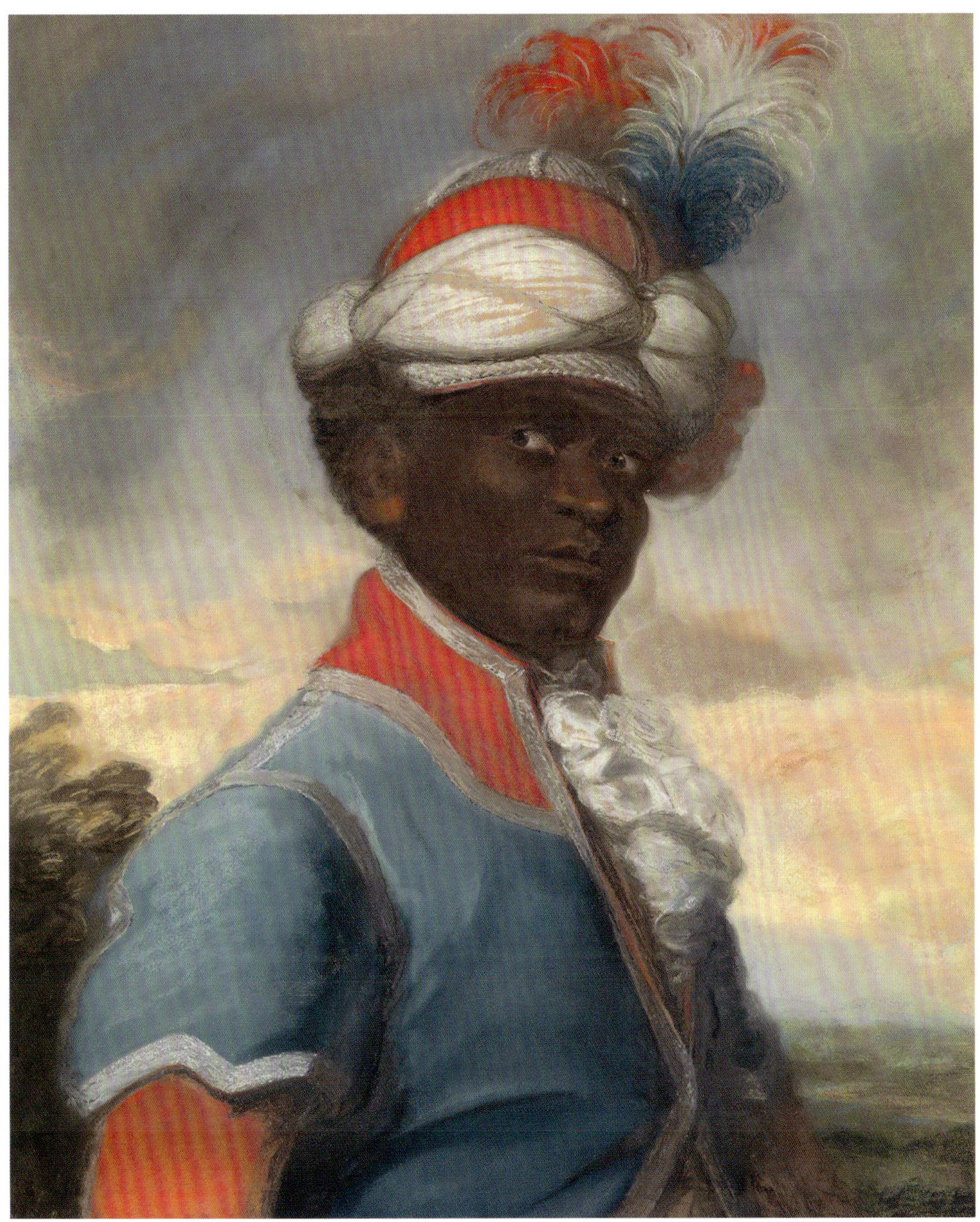

John Everett Millais 1829–96
The Yeoman of the Guard 1876
Oil paint on canvas 139.7 × 111.8

Millais's painting is an image of John Montague, who was made a Yeoman of the Guard after serving in the 16th Lancers in British India. The Yeomen of the Guard are the ceremonial bodyguards of the British monarch, initially formed by Henry VII in the wake of the 1485 Battle of Bosworth Field.

The Battle of Bosworth Field marked, for all intents and purposes, the end of the War of the Roses, a civil war between the houses of York and Lancaster. As the victor, Henry Tudor took the English throne, becoming the first Tudor monarch. Though the Tudor era would be one of stability and continuity, this was not clear in the immediate aftermath of the Battle of Bosworth Field. As such, when creating the uniform for his official bodyguards, the Yeomen of the Guard, Henry Tudor ensured they were laced with Tudor propaganda. Immediately beneath the collar, in pride of place on the front and back of the yeoman's torso, is an embroidered Tudor crown; below this are a Tudor rose, a shamrock and a thistle. Given that the shamrock and the thistle are recognisable emblems of Ireland and Scotland, respectively, their accompaniment with the Tudor rose furthers the notion that the Tudors are or should be synonymous with England. The design is completed by the monarch's initials sitting either side of a hawthorn bush, the place where Richard III's crown was allegedly discovered after the battle and brought to Henry to indicate his true right of succession. Though today, the uniform that the Yeomen wear is recognisable as that of the 'Beefeaters' who are wardens of the Tower of London, the uniform itself contains many elements specific to the Tudor context from which it emerged, symbolic of the Tudor victory and Henry's right to rule.

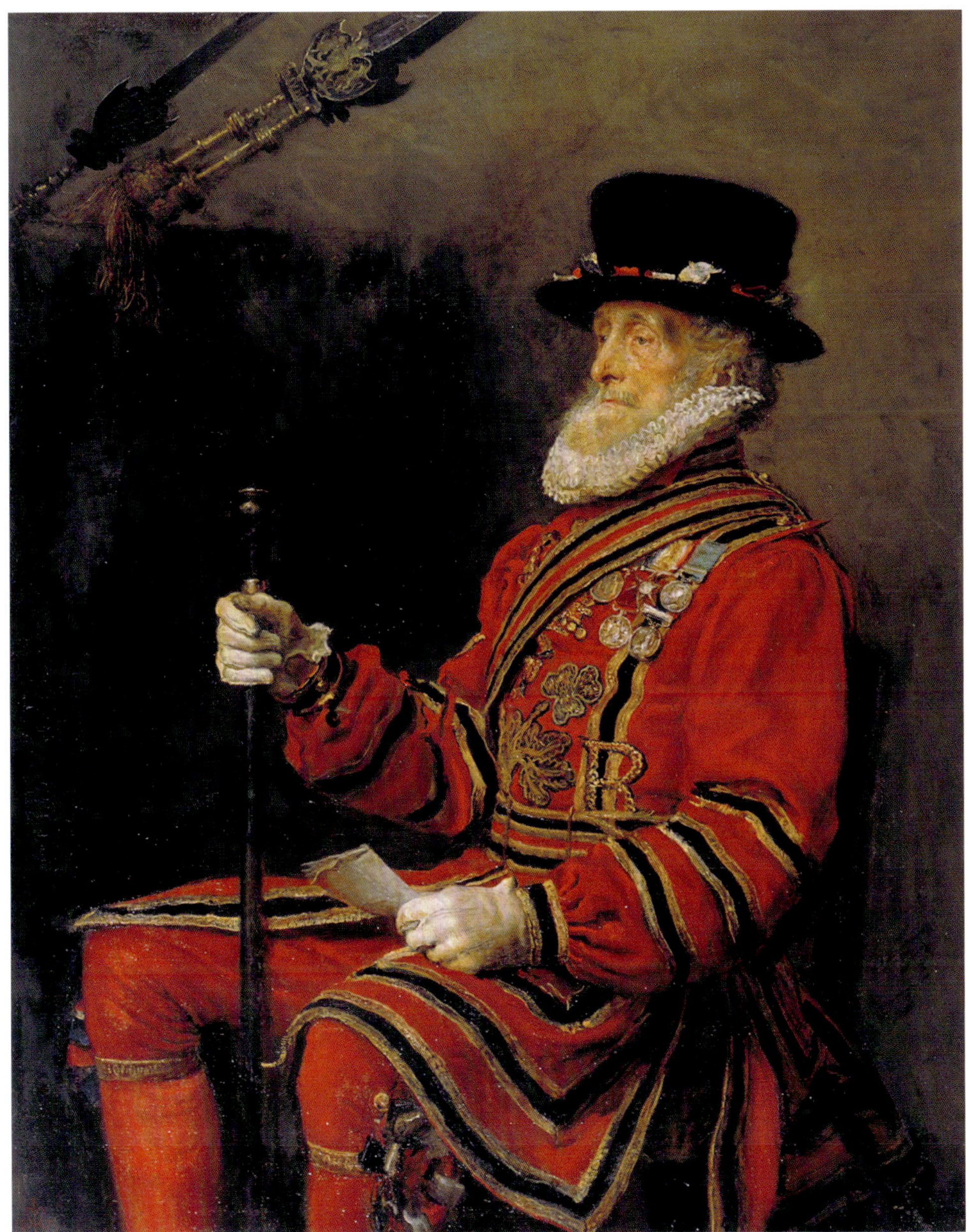

John Singer Sargent 1856–1925
Portrait of Ena Wertheimer: A Vele Gonfie 1904
Oil paint on canvas 163 × 108

Sargent paints Ena Wertheimer playfully posing in a shiny black cloak. A full sleeve pokes out beneath her gloved hand and a grandly plumed hat adds drama and contrast to her tightly styled hair. The cloak and hat are part of the traditional uniform of members of the Order of the Garter of the British monarchy, an order of chivalry and the most senior rank of knighthood, whose members are chosen personally by the sovereign.

Sargent displayed this work at the 1905 Royal Academy Summer Exhibition, submitting it with another work, *The Marlborough Family* 1905. A traditional formal family portrait, the painting shows the Marlboroughs posing together in full ceremonial regalia, which includes, for the Duke of Marlborough, his cloak and hat, signalling his membership of the Order of the Garter.

Ena Wertheimer was well known in the art world as the daughter of the middle-class Jewish art dealer Asher Wertheimer. In contrast to the Duke of Marlborough, however, she was not a current member of the Order. Not only that, Ena was distinctly ineligible for such a position. She was not from the landed gentry (the pool from which members of the Order were traditionally selected), she was a woman (the Order was a male preserve) and she was Jewish (the Order of the Garter had never admitted a Jewish person to its ranks). By showing the works alongside one another, Sargent posed a playful, yet serious challenge to the status quo. Even those who were unfamiliar with the specifics of the Order's dress could not fail to notice its use in Sargent's portrait of Ena, given its correct and expected inclusion in *The Marlborough Family*, placing this violation of protocol and its resultant provocation (why not?) front and centre.

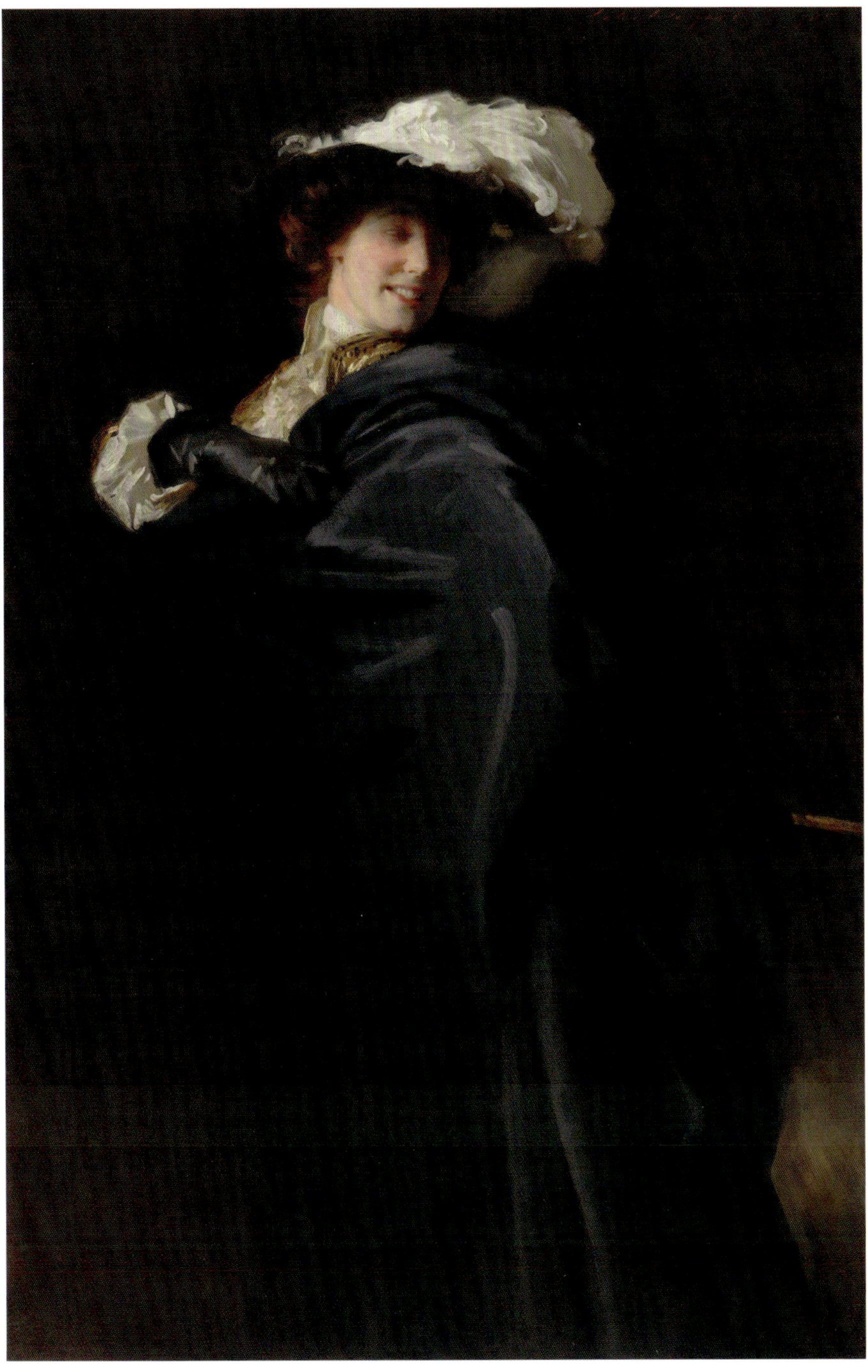

Sylvia Pankhurst 1882–1960
An Old-fashioned Pottery Turning Jasper-ware 1907
Gouache on paper 45.4 × 33.4

Women's rights activist and artist Sylvia Pankhurst created this work as part of her series *Women Workers of England*, documenting the working conditions and realities of women in the workplace during the first decade of the twentieth century. After completing her training at the Manchester Municipal School of Art and the Royal College of Art, London, Pankhurst set about employing her artistic skills to help advance the rights of women. In 1907, to that end, Pankhurst toured industrial sites and communities in the North of England.

Crucially for Pankhurst, the work shows male and female employees working together on the floor of a pottery. The woman operates the turner's lathe to ensure the pot rotates correctly, allowing the man to refine the work. This level of female submission troubled Pankhurst deeply, as the assignment of unskilled labour to women ensured their wages remained at a correspondingly low level.

The work documents two distinct fashions: that of a luxurious penchant for a distinct style of pottery – jasperware – and the ongoing attempts by women to navigate modesty and practicality in their work attire. Although the man in the image wears practical trousers, a shirt covered with a small apron and a cap, his female co-worker dons a full dress that, though fully appropriate for going to and from work, restricts movement and comfort. The only adjustment she has been able to make to her outfit is a large overall to shield the dress from dirt.

The popularity of jasperware – introduced in 1774 by entrepreneur and potter Josiah Wedgwood for production only in his Stoke-on-Trent factory – soon spread widely. It began to be produced by other potteries to serve those who wished for a piece without the price tag of the original. In the early twentieth century, demand for jasperware was as high as ever.

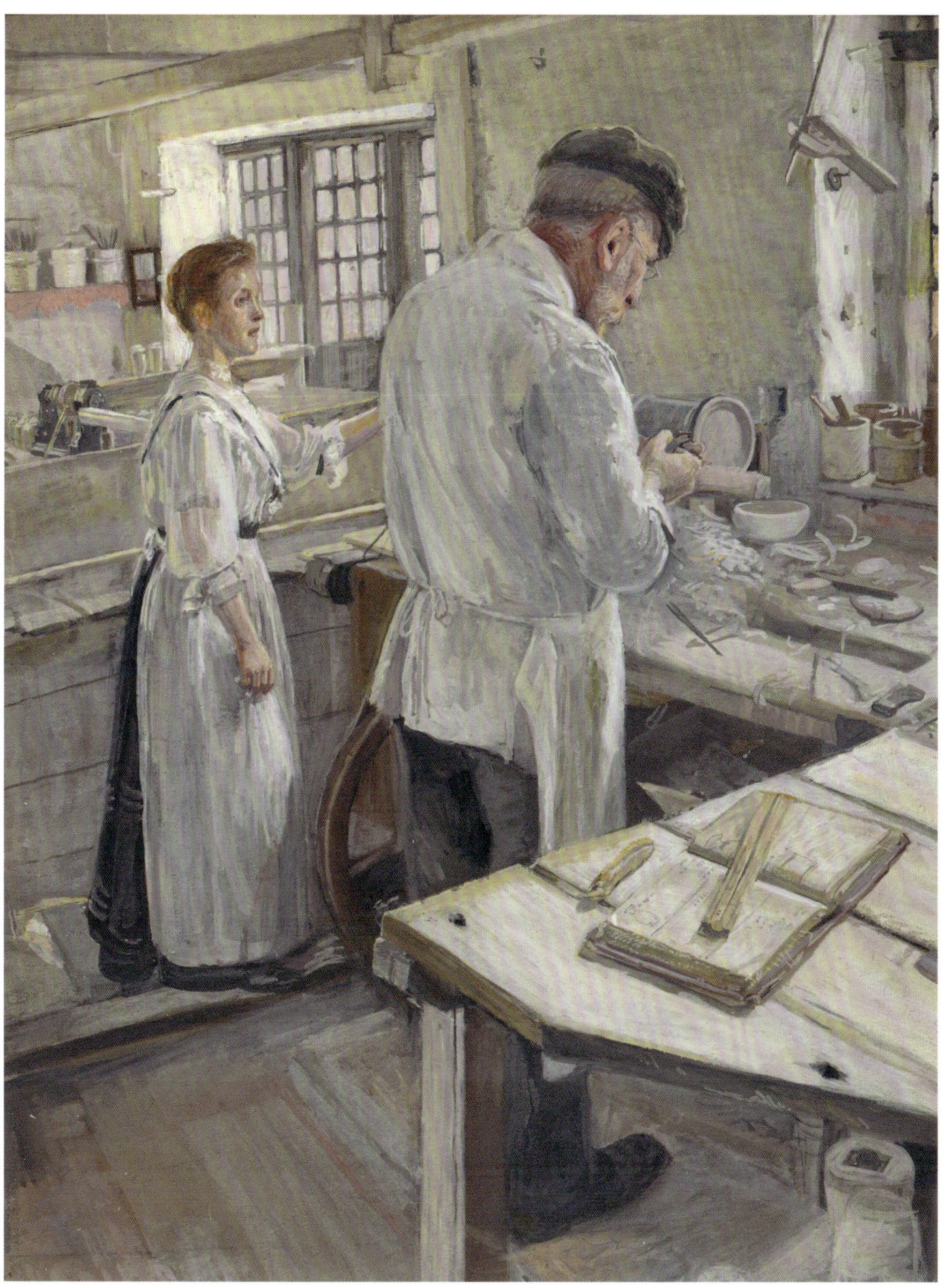

Augustus John 1878–1961
Woman Smiling 1908–9
Oil paint on canvas 196 × 98.2

In *Woman Smiling*, John paints his then mistress, and later common-law wife, Dorelia McNeill. Sitting against a drab brown background accented only with a grey throw over the chair she sits upon, McNeill's colourful clothing and bright smile jump off the canvas. She is dressed in a loose, uncorseted, buttoned dress, which is open at the collar. Her hair is covered by a headscarf which, like the dress, is a garment typically worn by Romany women in the UK in the beginning of the twentieth century.

John first encountered Romany culture when he was teaching painting in Liverpool. There, he met John Sampson, who was a Rai, and became fascinated by what he saw as a countercultural lifestyle. Sampson took John to visit the travelling communities of Cabbage Hall, near Aintree; after this encounter, John started wearing clothes that were traditionally associated with travelling communities, though with some artistic license and flourish. He learned the English dialect of Romani and began to spend his holidays and free time visiting different groups of travellers around the UK, dressing and living like them during his stays. McNeill would often join him on these trips, and this painting captures the lifestyle and uniform that she would adopt once she became John's primary romantic partner.

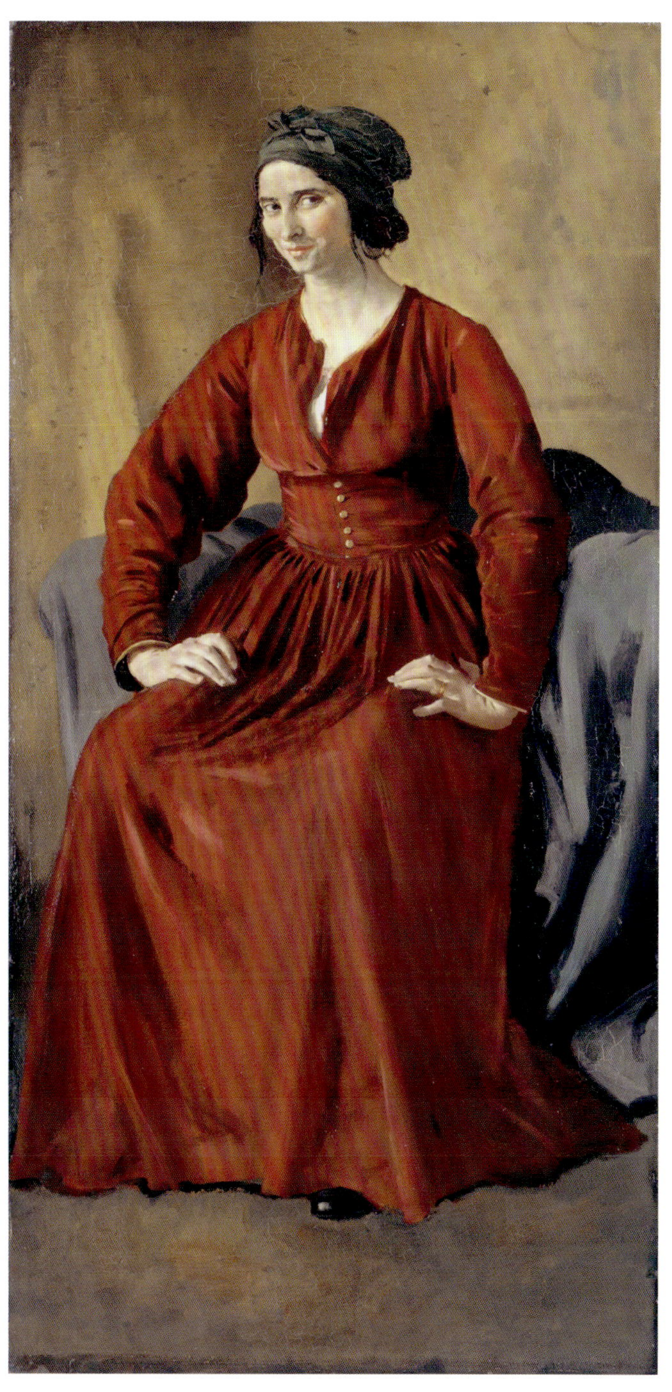

Christopher Richard Wynne Nevinson 1889–1946
La Mitrailleuse 1915
Oil paint on canvas 61 × 50.8

Wynne Nevinson painted this depiction of soldiers at the front while he was on leave from fighting in the First World War, during his honeymoon. During the earlier years of the war, there was a lot of discussion about uniforms among the allied forces. The French nature of this title – *La Mitrailleuse* is French for machine gun – indicates what a contemporary viewer would have understood immediately upon seeing the work: that the soldiers in the painting are French, not British. Though the French were the first army to form an official camouflage unit in 1915, they wore colourful uniforms as a matter of course. The red trousers and blue jackets were part of the uniform with which the French army began the war, while their British counterparts wore a drab military khaki from head to toe.

Throughout the war, therefore, while the British wished to convince their allies of the strategic advantage of a less colourful uniform, there was a lot of general discussion about uniform modernisations that might help the war come to an end sooner. In 1901, Thomas Burberry had submitted to the British Army's War Office for approval a design for a special raincoat for officers. Made from the waterproof gabardine fabric he had created a few decades earlier, the coat was double breasted and longer than was normal in both menswear and army uniform jackets. During the First World War, soldiers of officer class were permitted to wear these new waterproof coats. As they became particularly popular during the extended trench-based fighting, the coats came to be known as trench coats. After the war, many officers did not wish to cease wearing their trench coats during British rain showers, and the Burberry trench coat became part of mainstream British menswear.

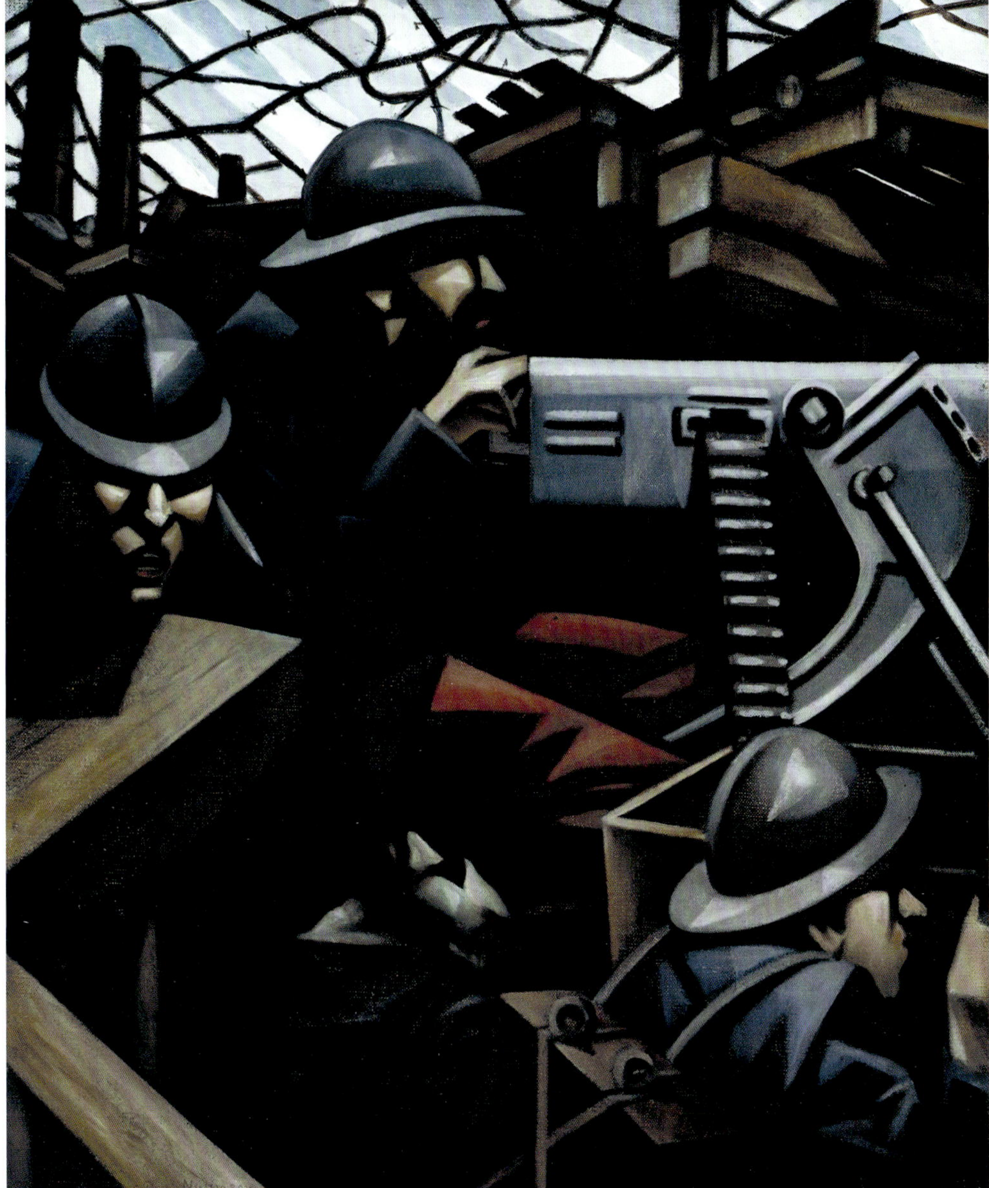

Edith Tudor-Hart 1908–78
London Bus Conductor c.1930
Gelatin silver print on paper 26.3 × 34.2

In this work, a bus conductor is framed by the bus he works on. He wears the uniform of a London bus conductor in the 1930s: a peaked cap and a single-breasted jacket with a high collar. On one wrist is a bright armband for visibility at night. Though the peaked cap was a popular choice of headwear among the working classes in many other Western countries, this was not the case in Britain, where that honour was held by the woollen flat cap. In Britain, the peaked caps worn by transport conductors conjured up images of army soldiers, who wore similar caps as part of their uniforms. The use of this style of cap gives the conductor the air of a foot soldier, albeit of London's bus network.

Born in Vienna to a Jewish family, Tudor-Hart trained under Walter Gropius at the Bauhaus school and became a photographer. She concentrated her camera lens on working-class subjects, channelling her communist beliefs into her work. In 1933, she moved to London in order to escape the rise of Nazism in her home country. After the Second World War, Tudor-Hart continued to pursue her photographic career, but also became involved in serious espionage. Given her communism, she supported the nascent Soviet Union and worked for them as a spy, recruiting the Cambridge Five, among others, as Soviet spies. This image of a London bus conductor combines these two strands of Tudor-Hart's pursuits: it concentrates on the realities of a working-class individual, but also captures a figure who, due to his uniform, maintains the anonymity and inconspicuous power that would make him an ideal spy.

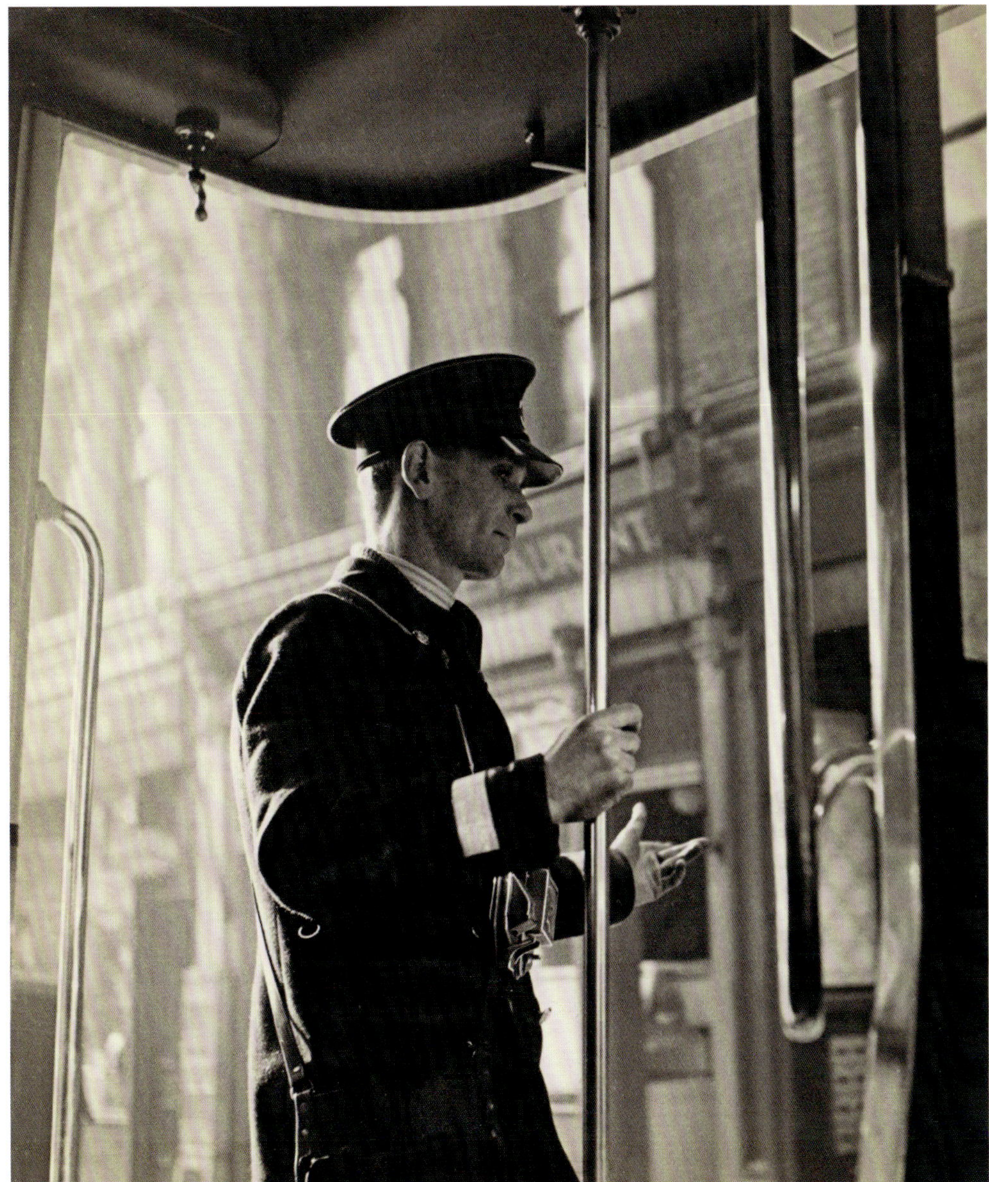

Diane Arbus 1923–71
Santas at the Santa Claus School, Albion, NY 1964
Gelatin silver print on paper 36.2 × 36.7

Much of American photographer Diane Arbus's practice concentrated upon the edges of American society. Her works from the 1960s brought together aspects of photojournalism and traditional portraiture with an ironic twist. Arbus took this image at the upstate New York Charles W. Howard Santa Claus School. Frustrated with the lack of professionalism he saw among men dressing up as Santa around the Christmas holidays, Charles W. Howard established the school in 1937 in order to train Santas to a higher standard. His concept was successful and thriving by the time Arbus visited in the 1960s.

Though he doesn't feature in the Christian Bible, this American version of Santa Claus is one of the most famous figures associated with Christmas globally today, recognisable by his unique red uniform of fur-trimmed coat, nightcap and long white beard. Prior to 1931, images of Santa showed him wearing a variety of outfits and appearing in various forms, from elf to human, man to boy. Everything changed when illustrator Haddon Sundblom created this incarnation of Santa for a national American campaign for Coca-Cola. Inspired by Clement Clarke Moore's poem 'A Visit from St. Nicholas', Sundblom wished to create a version of Santa Claus who exuded charm, warmth and a touch of mischief. Sundblom's creation was popular with consumers and company executives alike, and Coca-Cola commissioned him to create new advertisements featuring this version of Santa in the run-up to Christmas every year. By 1937, when Howard founded his Santa School, there was already only one acceptable version of Santa's outfit: the one peddled by Coca-Cola that persists to this day.

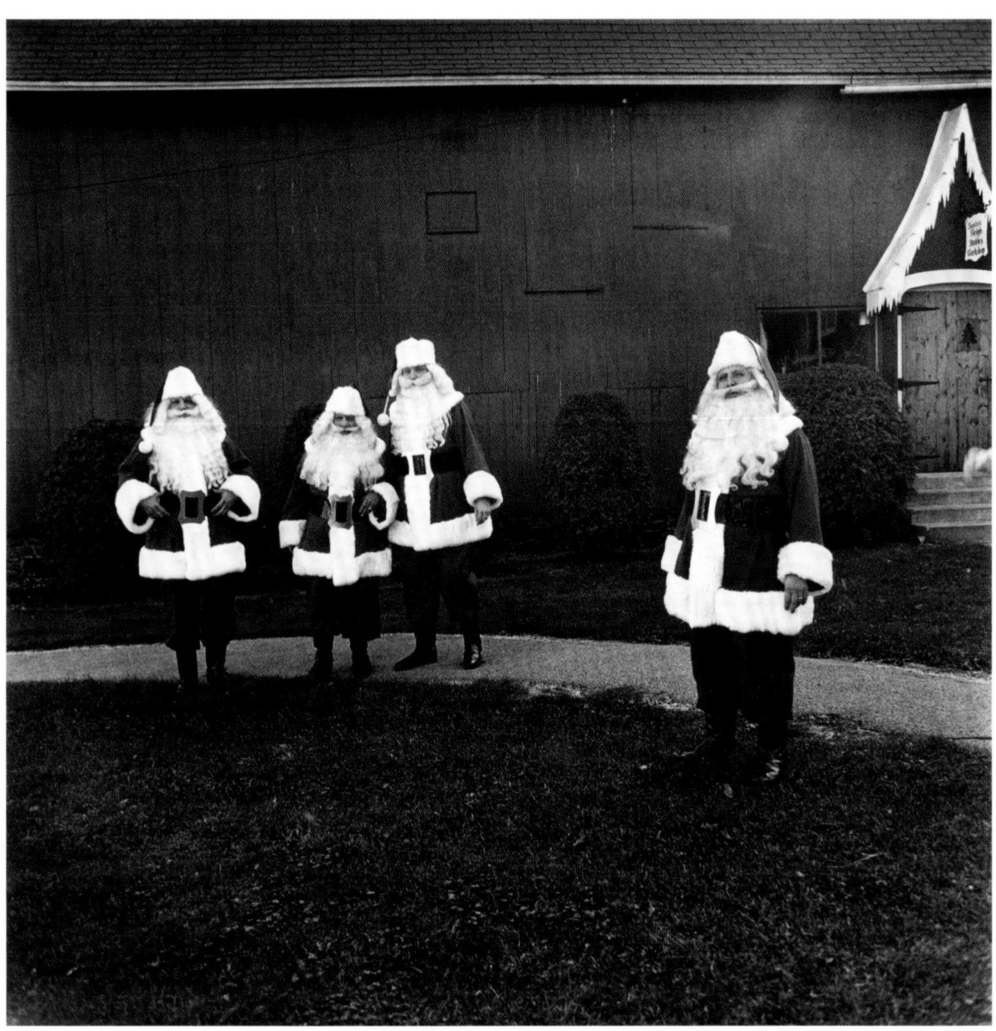
Santa's
Sleigh
Stables
Workshop

Jeanloup Sieff 1933–2000
English Nanny, England 1965
Gelatin silver print on paper 30.5 × 19.9

In Sieff's photograph, a stern-looking older woman stands immediately in front of the camera's lens, taking up the majority of the image. She is wearing all black. Her head is covered in a black flowing fabric similar to that of a nun's habit, her shoulders by a cape and her hands with black gloves. Behind her, standing before the house's front door, is a younger woman. Dressed in lighter colours and with head uncovered, she stands in a relaxed manner. Between the two women is a baby carriage, whose handles the younger woman is holding.

As the photograph's title suggests, the sterner woman in the foreground is the nanny. In England, nannies had initially been part of the cadre of servants in the employ of an aristocratic family. In the nineteenth century, formal training for nannies emerged in the form of training colleges, such as the famous Norland Institute, which sought to professionalise the occupation. Part of this involved a wish to elevate the status of the nanny above parlourmaid, and this led to the introduction of uniforms specific to each individual college. As a French photographer, Sieff may have found the particularly English phenomenon of nannies having uniforms outdated or strange, and the composition of his photograph speaks of an uneasy imbalance between the two women.

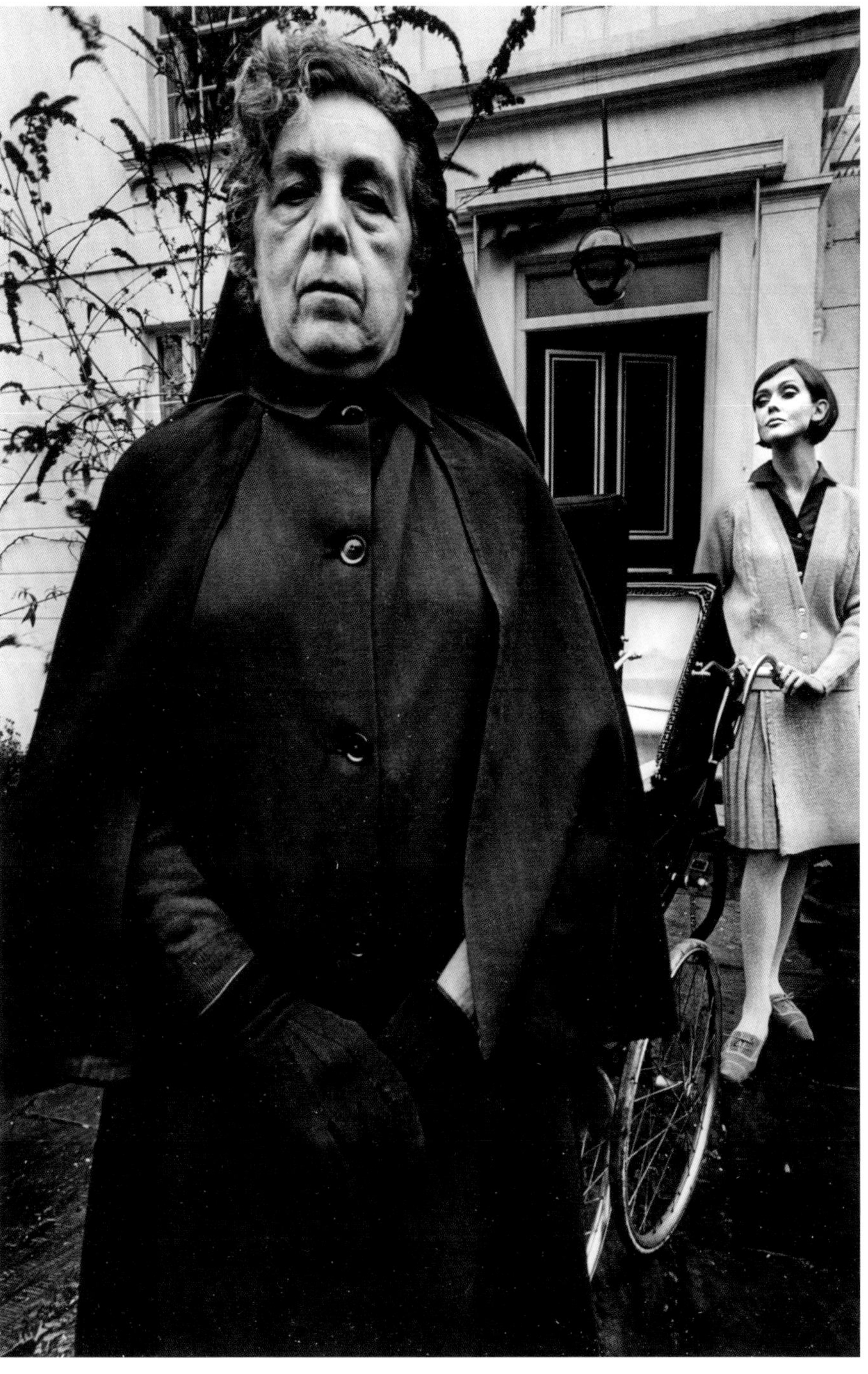

Paula Rego 1935–2022
Bride 1994
Pastel on paper on aluminium 120 × 160.6

Rego's painting almost pulsates with emotion. The sitter's inscrutable expression is enhanced and made of further importance by her white dress and white veil, which signify that she is a bride and is, therefore, either just married or about to be married. Though the white dress is today a signifier of bridal identity in many countries across the globe, this is a very modern convention begun in the nineteenth century in the wake of the wedding of Queen Victoria of Britain to her cousin, Albert.

In 1840, at a slightly precarious time for the British monarchy, Queen Victoria was married in a more public manner than her predecessors. She processed publicly through the streets on the way to the church and, in order to utilise this public relations opportunity further, the royal family ensured wide global press coverage of the ceremony. Victoria wore a white dress made of Spitalfields silk and Honiton lace, choosing to forgo the red ermine robe that she was expected, by protocol, to wear at formal occasions. Until this time, the colour of wedding dresses was completely dependent upon the choice of the bride and the available fabrics. However, as newspapers reported on the Queen's choice not to dress in keeping with protocol, they concentrated on the whiteness of the dress she chose. Brides across the world were influenced by the idea when reading coverage of the event and adopted white for their own wedding days – a practice almost ubiquitous today.

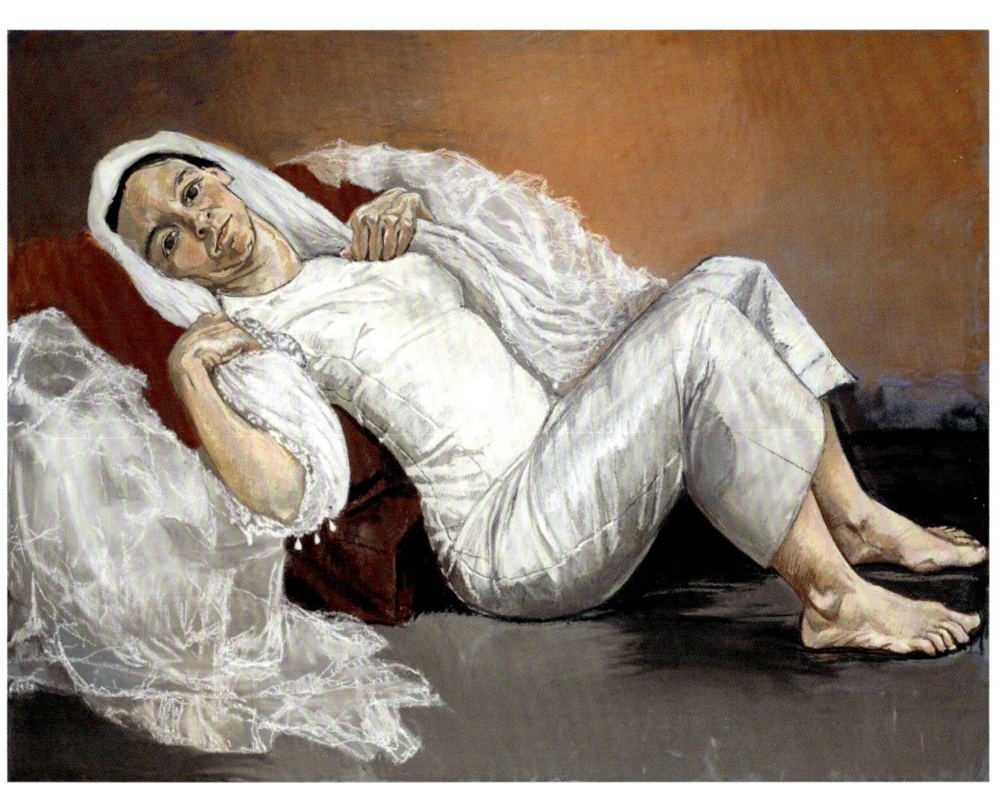

Martin Parr 1952–
GB, England, Epsom. The Derby, 2004 2004
From the series *Luxury*
Inkjet print on paper, mounted on aluminium 70.6 × 50.4

This work was initially created as part of Martin Parr's photobook *Luxury*. Published in 2009, one year after the 2008 financial crash, the series explores the excesses and absurdities of wealth, captured during a time of immense global hardship and inequality. This image was taken at the Epsom Derby, a horse racing event in England. Instead of capturing the race itself, Parr turns his camera towards its observers, who are decked out in all their finery.

All the male subjects wear top hats, ties and jackets. Though the boy in the foreground is seated, making it impossible to determine the precise style of his jacket, the two men who stand in the background are wearing clearly identifiable morning suits. Indeed, formal day dress, the dress code of Epsom's Derby Day, requires that morning suit and top hat be worn. Though nowadays seen as part of formal dress, the morning suit itself developed in the nineteenth century, when gentlemen customarily wore long frock coats during the day. Such strictures were not particularly practical for those who were avid horse riders, and people started to wear jackets that were cut away at the front with a deep slit at the back, allowing the two sides (or 'tails') to fall either side of the horse they were riding. By the early twentieth century, this adjusted formal wear had taken over as the dominant formal attire in Western dress. Fittingly, it is still worn today by those dressing up to watch British horse races, even though they may be unaware of the jacket's sport-related origins. Parr's emphasis on the costume and the serious young boy in Epsom enhance the irony of his social commentary.

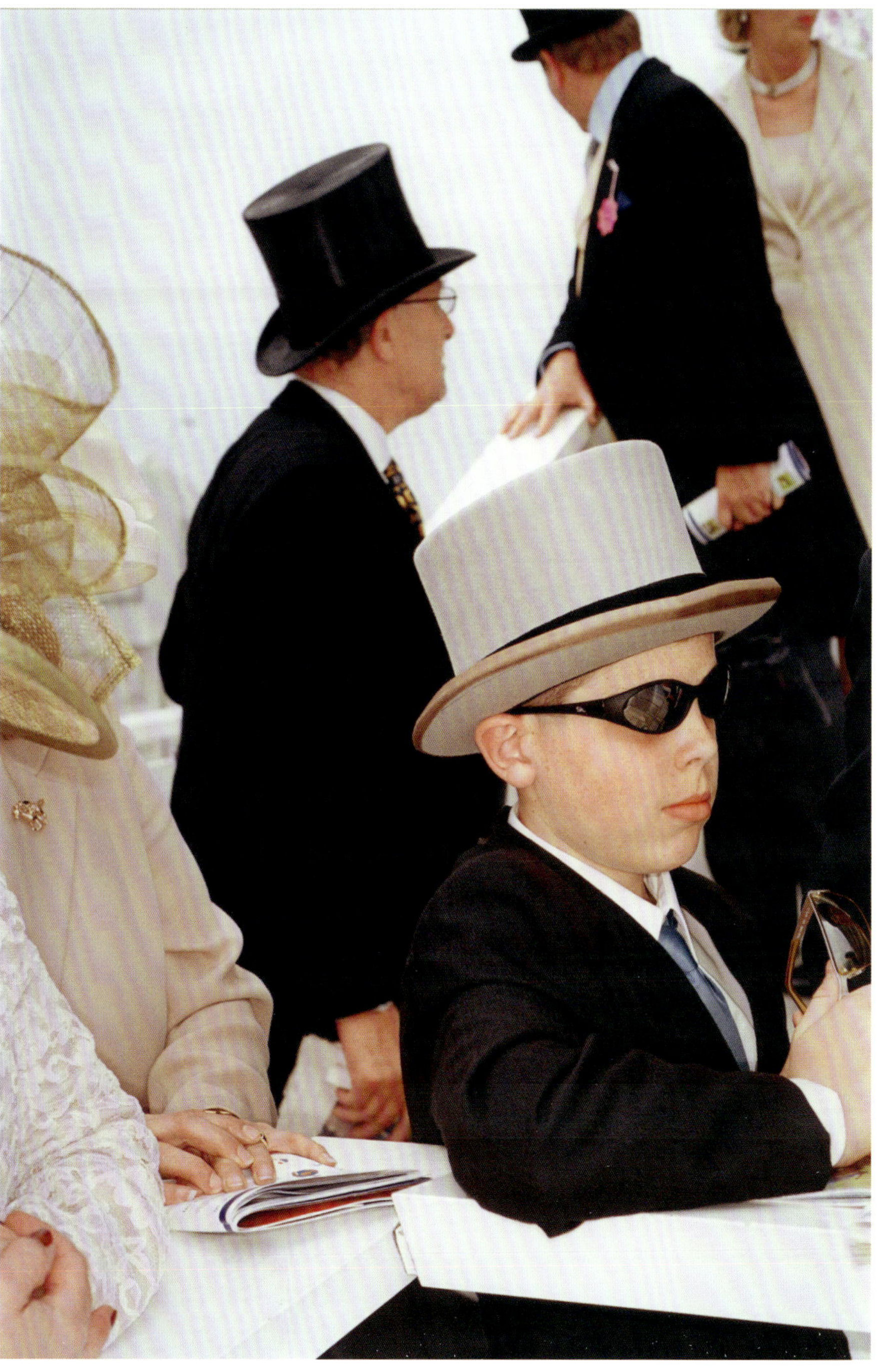

Zanele Muholi 1972–
In-security 2003
From the series *Only Half the Picture* 2003–6
Gelatin silver print on paper 48.2 × 33.2

Muholi's photograph hails from a series of eight images of lesbian women, none of which show the subject's head, leaving them unidentifiable and anonymous. Nonetheless, each image includes enough details to build a sense of drama and pathos, encouraging the viewer to care for and empathise with the unknown figure.

In-security shows more of the subject's body than most of the works in the series, though, unlike in many other images in the series, the subject here is fully dressed. Their lace up black boots are recognisable as combat boots, while the full military-style short-sleeved overall, lacking military paraphernalia, indicates they work as some sort of security guard. The outfit, like that of many security professionals, gains a visual gravitas and authority from its proximity to standard issue army uniform. The authority and power of private security forces in post-apartheid South Africa is extremely intimidating, yet there is also something vulnerable about the subject's cross-armed stance.

Muholi describes their practice as a form of 'visual activism'. As a series, these images are intended to accentuate the plight, discrimination against and struggle of Black lesbian women. Writing of their work at the conclusion of this series, Muholi powerfully declared: 'This is a time for a visual state of emergence. The preservation and mapping of our herstories is the only way for us black lesbians to be visible.' With the intimidating overtones of the subject's uniform in *In-security*, Muholi presents a nuanced range of realities, refusing to sanitise and sweeten their subjects or their lives.

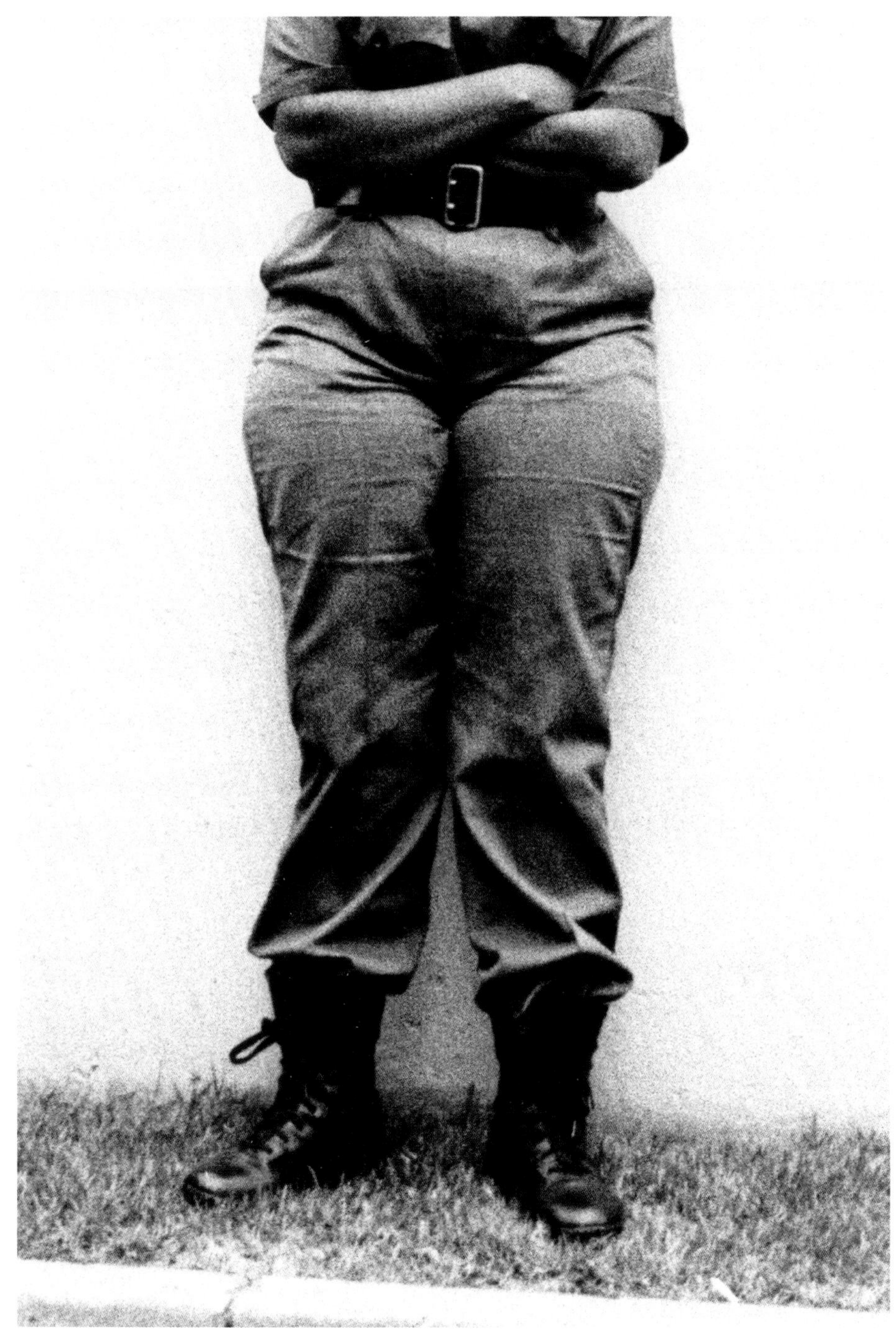

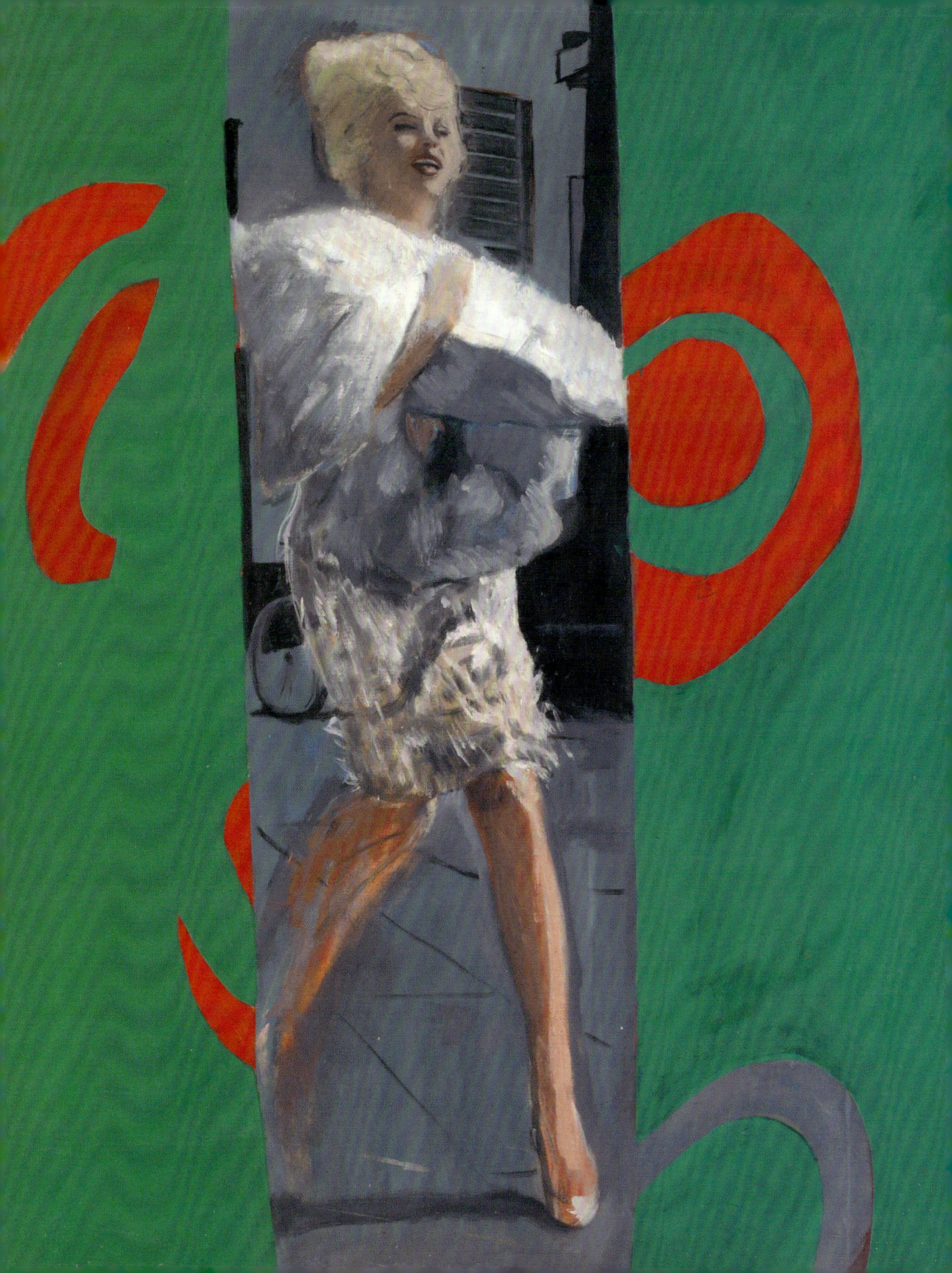

Swinging Sixties

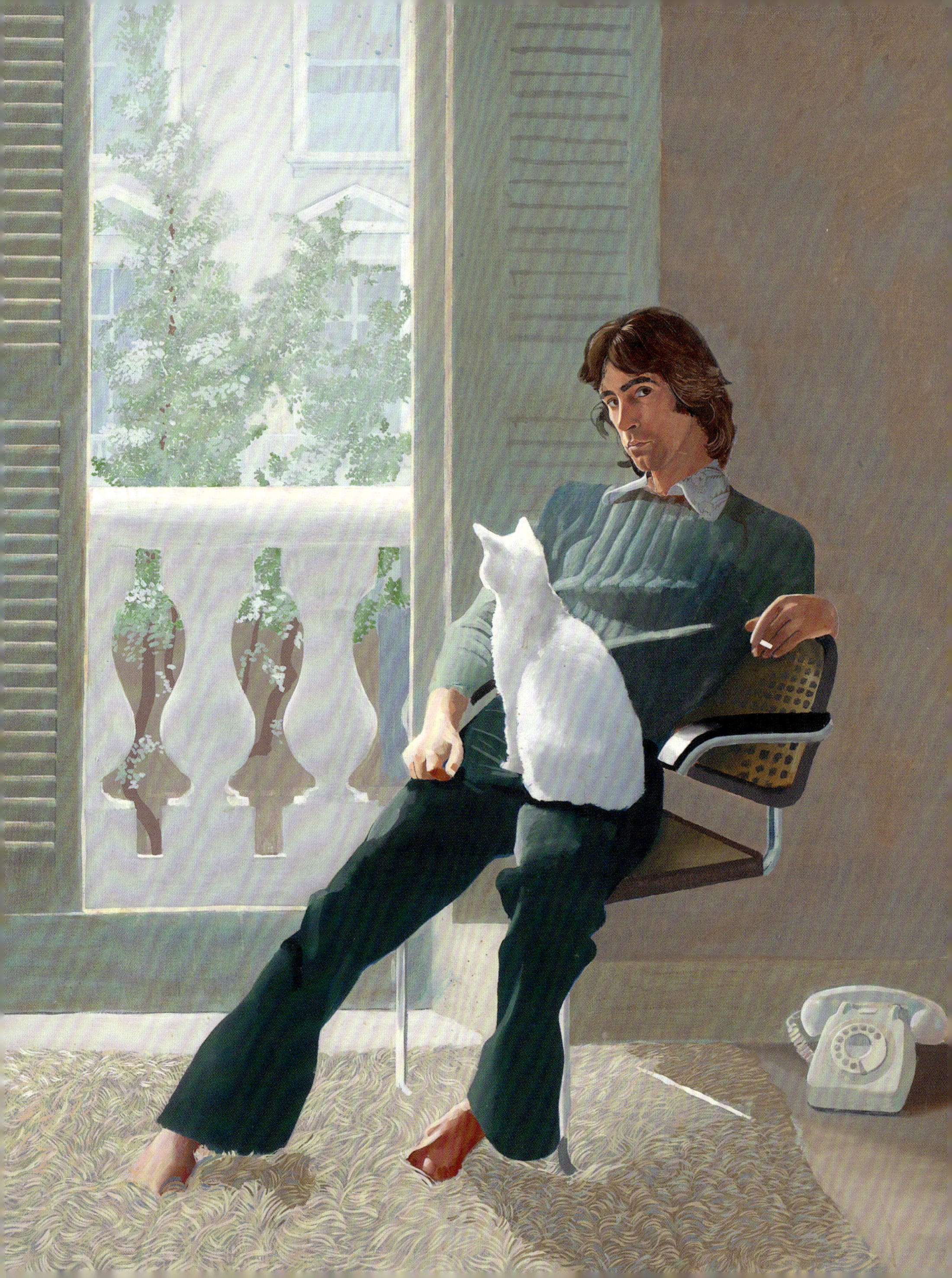

The 1960s saw a surge of modern cultural activity and celebration in Britain. Many Britons, particularly young ones, felt a sudden giddy excitement in the wake of the final and complete lifting of post-war rations and the subsequent boost to the British economy and everyday living. Britain had experienced a post-war baby boom and, in the 1960s, this cohort of babies reached their teen years at a particularly auspicious time. The term 'swinging' was 1960s English slang for trendy and was a phrase a number of people used to describe the mid-1960s cultural resurgence. After visiting in 1965, American *Vogue* editor Diana Vreeland wrote that 'London is the most swinging city in the world at the moment', a phrase that ended up sticking, and London's cultural rejuvenation became known as the 'Swinging Sixties'.

The fulcrum of the Swinging Sixties scene was the raucous parties at which one could enjoy the two major cultural elements of the moment: revolutionary music and envelope-pushing fashion. British bands such as The Beatles, The Kinks and The Rolling Stones enjoyed immense global fame and celebrity status. Dressed in the fashions that were being pioneered by boutiques on the King's Road in London's Chelsea neighbourhood (such as the miniskirt and, later, the minidress), these musical acts ensured that the dress trends of Britain spread with similar virality. British fashion model Twiggy also reached an international level of fame: her short hair, extremely long 'twiggy' legs, large eyes and long eyelashes gave her a unique and timely appearance that came to epitomise the beauty as well as fashion trends of the time.

This chapter looks at artists who played with, participated in and reacted to this unique cultural moment. For some of them, the excitement and verve of the moment invigorated them with a new-found sense of cultural freedom; for others, particularly the women artists featured, the freedom of others forced them to confront how trapped they felt on a personal level.

David Hockney *Mr. and Mrs. Clarke and Percy* 1970–1 (detail, see p.109). •
Page 90: Pauline Boty *The Only Blonde in the World* 1963 (detail, see p.99)

Peter Blake 1932–
On the Balcony 1955–7
Oil paint on canvas 121.3 × 90.8

After the Second World War, most of the Allied Forces nations were rebuilding their destroyed cityscapes in the midst of ongoing rationing. The United States, however, was relatively unscathed, which allowed for the emergence of its government and economy as a global powerhouse. In Britain, during the first two decades after the war, many residents developed a particular fascination with the wealth and attendant materialism they could only access through hard-to-come-by American magazines. While most of the West struggled with interrupted supply chains for basic amenities, suburban households throughout the United States were buying their own washing machines, tumble dryers and even fitted kitchens.

As an artist, Peter Blake was particularly fascinated with the visual component of this new-found material wealth. Cutting through a deep-seated division between so-called 'high' and 'low' culture, he began to incorporate elements of American magazine culture into his paintings, arguing for the demolition of a hierarchy of aesthetic culture he felt did not accurately reflect his own experiences. Containing twenty-seven visual variations of its title, *On the Balcony* makes explicit this fusion of the popular and the elite. Press images of the royal family waving from the balcony run across the canvas alongside a reproduction of Édouard Manet's *The Balcony* 1868–9. Young people dressed in contemporary clothing populate the work in static poses, allowing the array of visual sources to flow and float in, around and even over them: the head of one sitter is obscured beneath a copy of *LIFE* magazine. The cover image, from the 5 August 1957 edition of the publication, belongs to a story about 'London's Social Scene: The Most Lavish in Years'. Blake's inclusion of the image is indicative of an exciting shift that was occurring – the emergence of a cultural scene in London so interesting that even the Americans deemed it worthy of coverage.

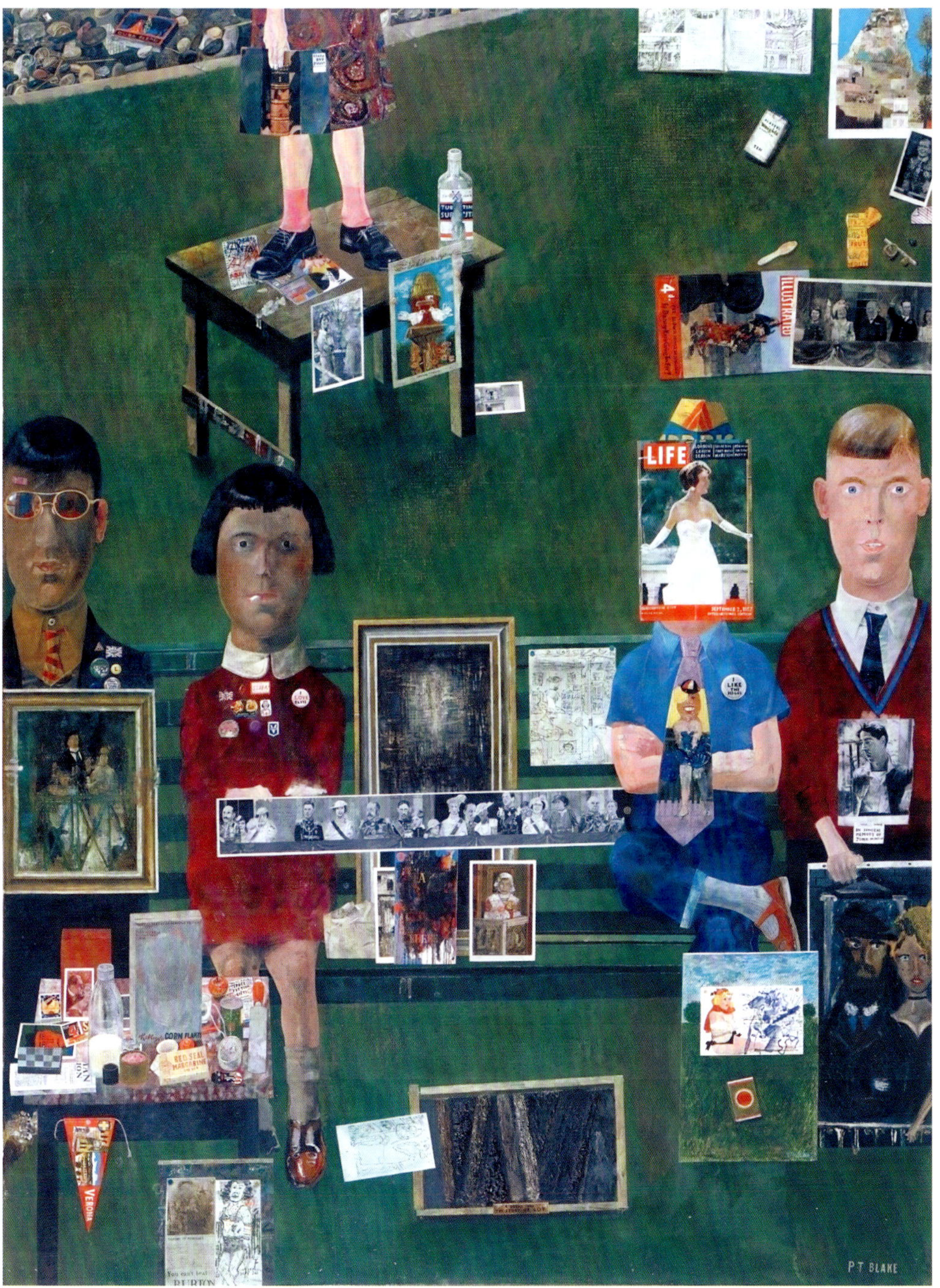
LIFE
ILLUSTRATED
CORN FLAKES
VERONA
P T BLAKE

Althea McNish 1924–2020
Van Gogh 1959
Screenprinted cotton 142.2 × 125.7

Born in Trinidad, Althea McNish moved to London in 1951 from Port of Spain, where she had already established her reputation as a promising junior member of the Trinidad Arts Society. After arriving in London, McNish enrolled on a printing course at the London School of Printing and Graphic Arts, after which she studied at Central School of Arts and Craft and undertook a postgraduate degree at the Royal College of Art. Arthur Stewart-Liberty, then chairman of the Liberty London department store, saw McNish's work at her graduation show and commissioned her to create designs for Liberty's fashion and furnishing fabric line.

McNish went on to create fabrics for some of the most famous textile producers in Britain, including Heal's (for whom she created *Van Gogh*) and Hull Traders, as well as French fashion houses Dior and Schiaparelli. McNish maintained a strong and proud Caribbean identity in the networks she fostered and the commissions she undertook. A founding member of the Caribbean Artists Movement, McNish designed fabrics for Elizabeth II to wear on her official visit to Trinidad and Tobago in 1966 in the aftermath of its independence.

Van Gogh can be read as a vital fusion of McNish's artistic influences. Bright washes of orange and pink dominate the background of the design, reminiscent of the brighter fabric colours that were prevalent in Trinidad during her upbringing. The carefully illustrated sunflowers hint at McNish's later, London-based formal artistic education, where the modernism of Dutch painters such as Van Gogh was taught as the ultimate in artistic sophistication. It is in this merging of influences that McNish's revolutionary nature lies. The power of this fusion is heightened by McNish's chosen art form, textile design – a form over which British companies and consumers had, for so long, exerted a colonial influence.

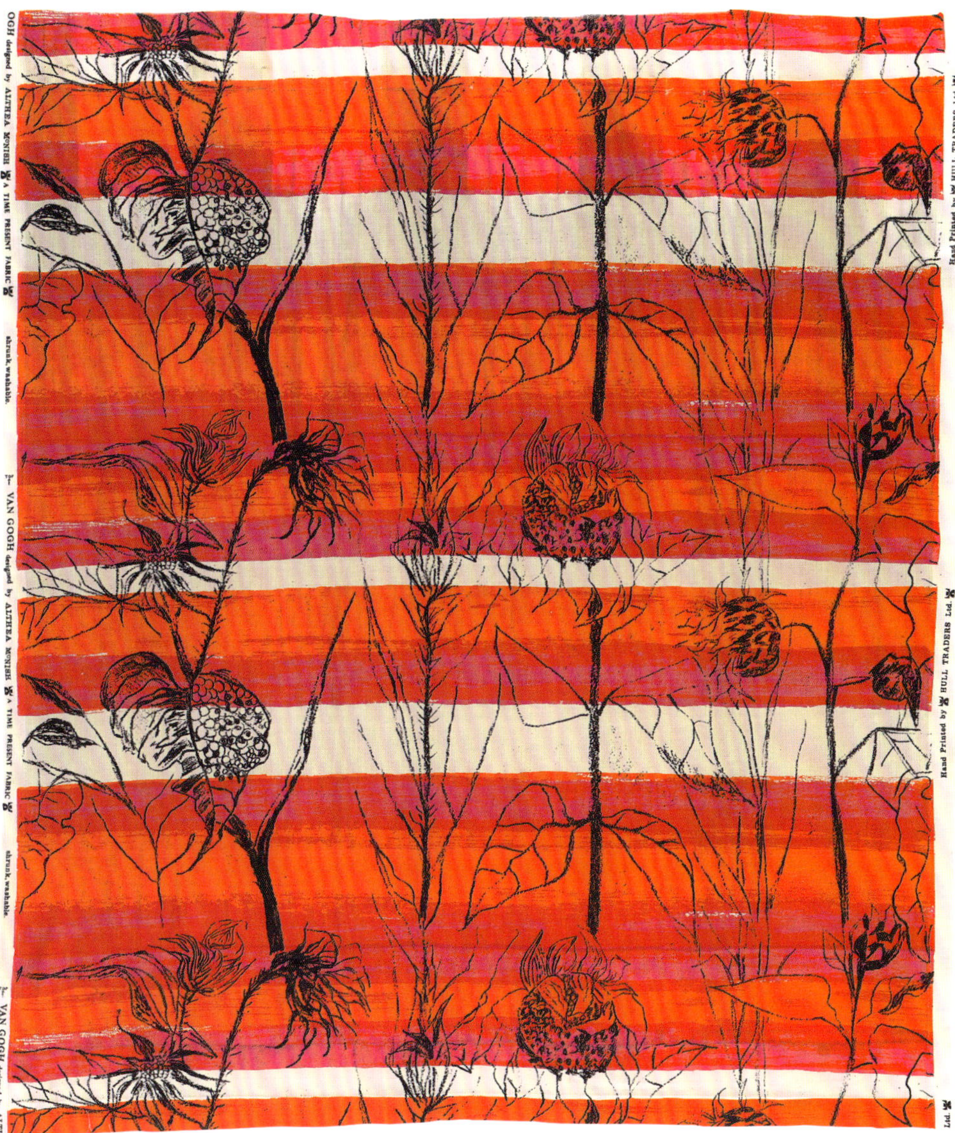
VAN GOGH designed by ALTHEA McNISH A TIME PRESENT FABRIC
shrunk, washable
Hand Printed by HULL TRADERS Ltd.

Pauline Boty 1938–66
The Only Blonde in the World 1963
Oil paint on canvas 122.4 × 153 × 2.5

The work's title, *The Only Blonde in the World*, refers to the trend of platinum blonde hair that American actress Marilyn Monroe pioneered. Though not the first blonde-haired starlet to capture Hollywood's imagination, Monroe took the colour to its extreme, dying her hair what she called 'pillow-case white'. Monroe's popularity coincided with Clairol's launch, in 1956, of the first at-home hair colouring system, Miss Clairol Hair Color Bath. Suddenly, Marilyn's bleached blonde look felt more attainable. The fashion for blonde locks took off globally, and women around the world, including the artist Pauline Boty, dyed their hair a vibrant blonde, attempting to emulate the starlet as well as the Hollywood glamour she personified.

Although consisting entirely of oil paint on canvas, *The Only Blonde in the World* employs a collage aesthetic reminiscent of print culture. A horizontal strip interrupts an otherwise bright abstract composition: monochromatic and cropped, it shows Marilyn Monroe in character as Sugar Kane from *Some Like it Hot* (1959). Boty completed the work in the year after Monroe's tragic death and this, combined with her choice to depict Monroe in costume as a character rather than as herself, imbues the work with pathos. Boty seems to be suggesting that the glamorous appearance of this blonde starlet is, itself, the ultimate performance – as natural as her hair colour.

Though Boty preferred to work as a painter, she applied to study stained glass at Wimbledon School of Art and the Royal College of Art after hearing that the discipline was less discriminatory against women. She continued with her painting practice upon graduation. Boty's struggles with the misogynistic nature of the art world in which she so desperately wanted to participate add another layer of poignancy to this depiction of a blonde starlet.

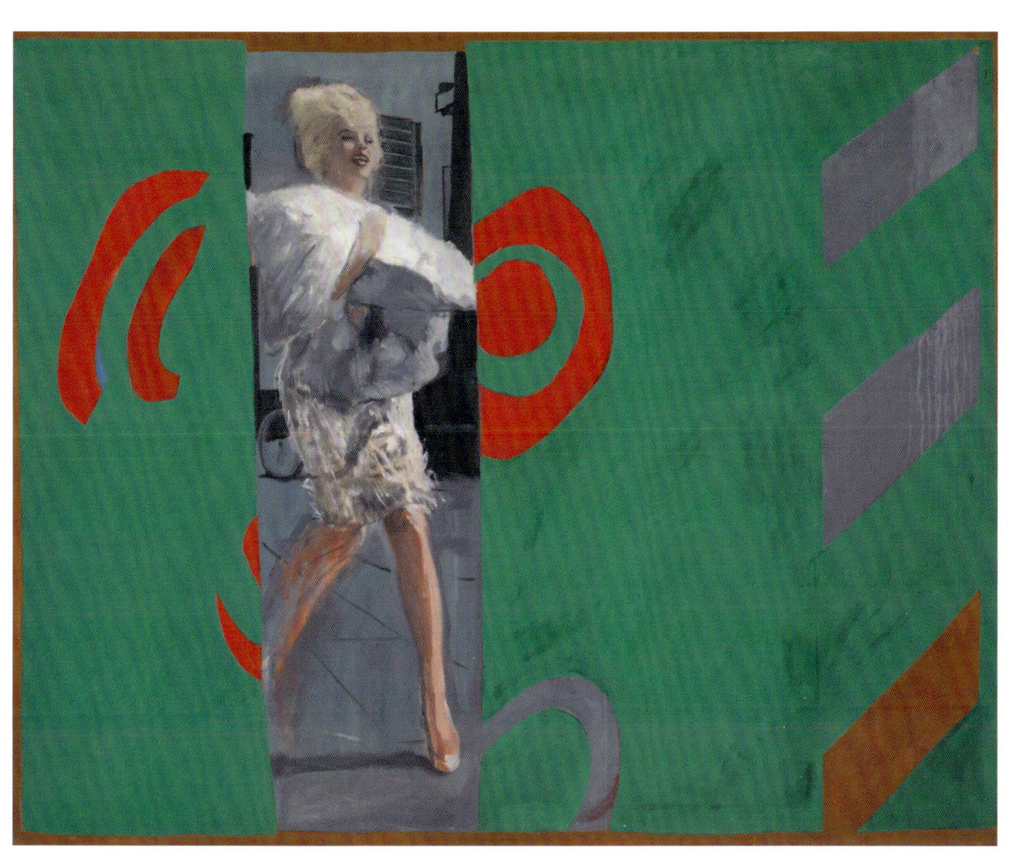

Bridget Riley 1931–
Fall 1963
Polyvinyl acetate paint on hardboard 141 × 140.3

Fall is a prime example of what came to be called op art, in which the entirety of the composition contrives to create an optical illusion and appears to the viewer to be moving, flowing or composed of forms which are not really present. The curved black-and-white lines – of various densities – in this work appear to 'fall' together, cascading down the canvas in an arrangement that creates the illusion of corresponding horizontal curves moving across the canvas against the dominant grain. At a time when many pop artists were taking the veracity of culturally recognisable visual motifs for granted and manipulating their meaning through clever juxtaposition, Riley used monochromatic curvilinear forms to question the boundaries and possibilities of vision and perception in a primarily cerebral manner.

After spending her childhood in Cornwall, Riley moved to London to attend boarding school and then stayed in the city to study art, first at Goldsmiths' College and then the Royal College of Art. Upon graduation, Riley initially worked as an art teacher, though she began to explore a painting career in earnest in the early 1960s. In 1962, Riley had her first solo show at Victor Musgrave's Gallery One, itself a centre of the 1960s cultural scene, in the heart of London's Soho. From then on, Riley's distinctive monochromatic illusionistic art style became synonymous with the Swinging Sixties, appearing as the backdrop to many fashion photoshoots for *Vogue* and other major print publications. Riley herself gained renown and appeared in *Vogue* in 1965, sandwiched between her own creations in a photograph by Lord Snowdon. From there, her success and public recognition grew, and she became the first woman to win the International Prize for Painting at the Venice Biennale in 1968.

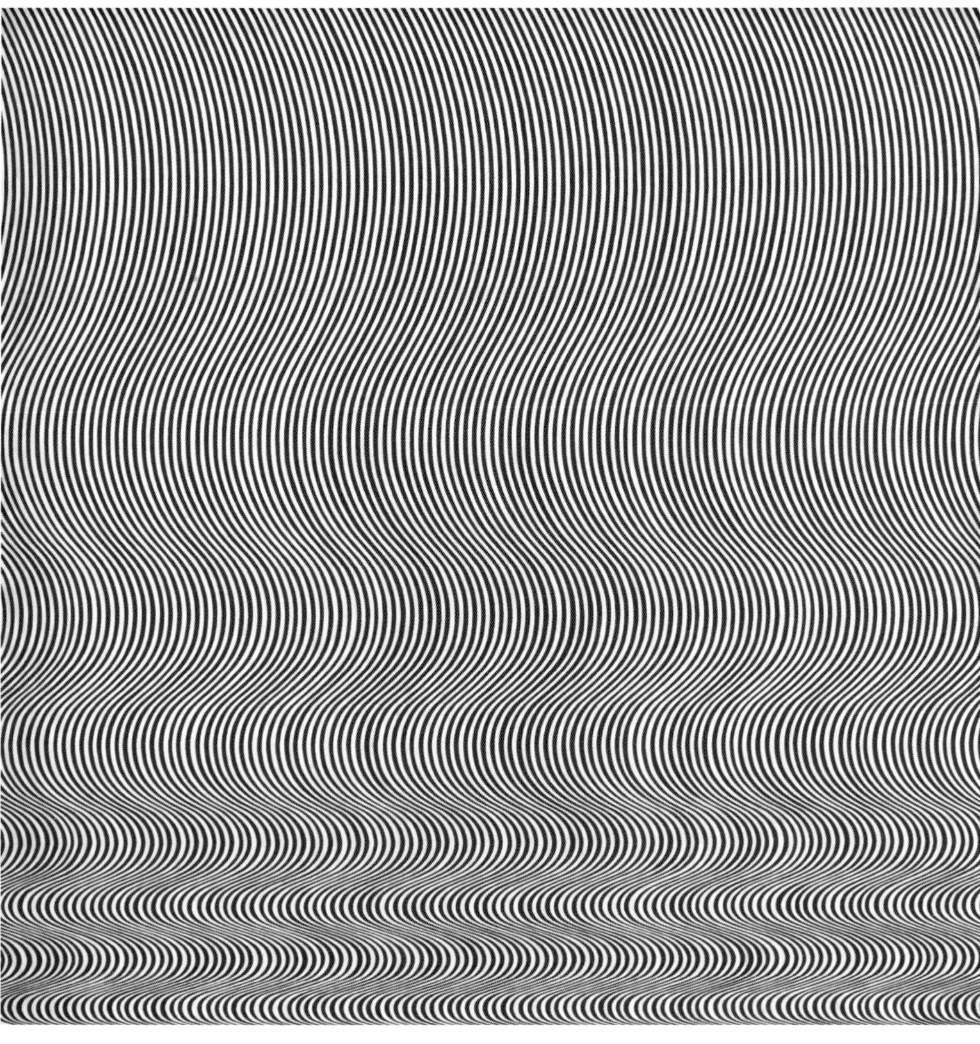

Yoko Ono 1933–
Still from *Cut Piece* 1964/5
Film, 16mm, shown as video, black and white, and sound (stereo), 8 min 27 sec

In 1964, emerging artist Yoko Ono performed the first iteration of her work *Cut Piece* in Kyoto (the 1965 performance in New York is pictured here). In the 'score' laying out the timing and actions of the work, akin to that of a piece of music, Ono described:

> Performer sits on stage with a pair of scissors in front of him. It is announced that members of the audience may come on stage – one at a time – to cut a small piece of the performer's clothing to take with them. Performer remains motionless throughout the piece. Piece ends at the performer's option.

The work begins in a rather slow manner, as one by one members of the audience work up the courage to approach the performer and use the scissors as suggested. In video recordings and accounts of the work by those present in the audience on the occasions Ono performed the work, the momentum of audience participants gradually builds, picking up in earnest at the precise moment Ono's clothing is diminishing.

Anticipating debates around the value, rights and boundaries of propriety for women that were to come to the front of social consciousness later in the decade, Ono outsources decisions about how to cover her body and how to relate to it to the audience members. At a certain point, they cut through intimate parts of Ono's clothing, including her bra straps. There is a suddenness to this violence, which has developed from the initially innocuous action of cutting swatches of cloth. In this, the role of clothing as both potential cover and means of exposure is underlined: in the face of determined violence against women, their power to protect themselves is rendered nul.

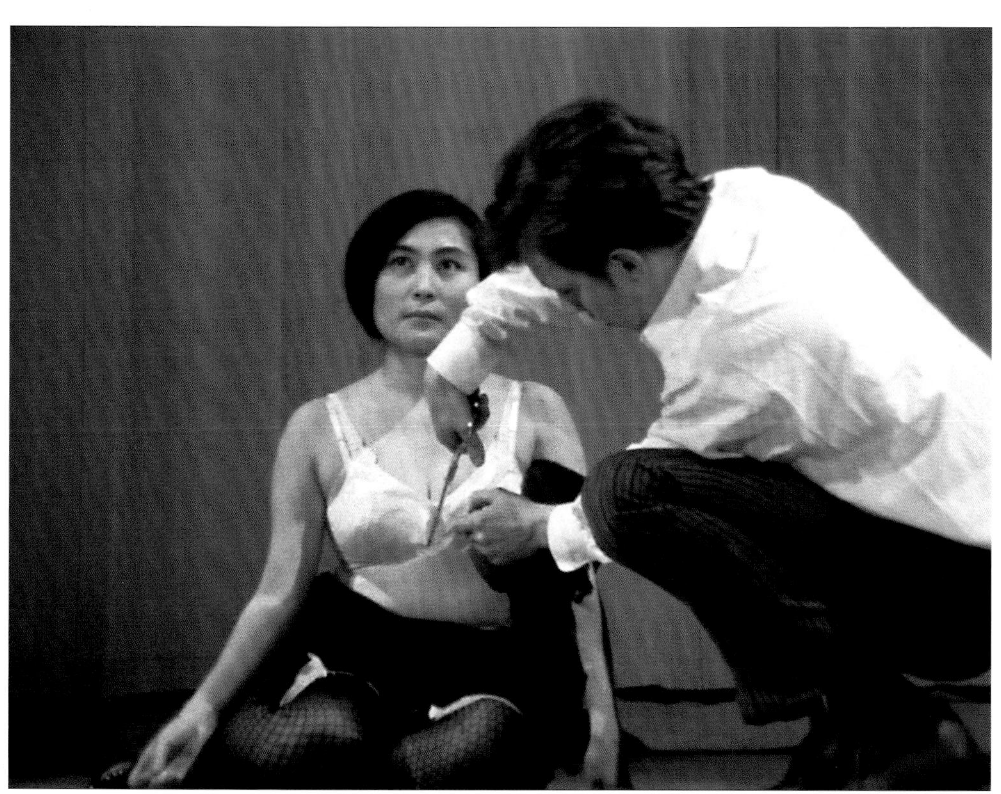

Dorothy Bohm 1924–
Chelsea, London 1968
Gelatin silver print on paper 21.2 × 11.5

As home to Mary Quant's King's Road shop Bazaar, Chelsea was the beating heart of the 1960s style of 'mod' dressing. Though capturing a young woman donning a distinctly contemporary minidress in one of the centres of this subculture, Bohm's photograph is not a typical portrait nor a fashion photograph. Its subject is off centre, framed by a doorway, a shop window and the shadow of some railings. It is almost an incidental element of the image's composition. For Bohm, it was important to capture the distinct flavour of London's neighbourhoods in her photography:

> Almost every area had its own character and I knew I was undertaking a very difficult task. I tried not to be content with just the facade or outward appearance of things. I hoped to penetrate just beyond that, to portray a living London: the people who pursued their daily occupations, walked, talked, ate or relaxed and dressed in the fashions of the time.[4]

Born in Konigsberg to a Jewish family, Bohm fled Nazi rule for England in 1939. Upon departure, her father had gifted her a Leica camera, and she soon developed a keen photographic eye. Once settled in England, Bohm studied photography at the Manchester College of Technology, before working in studio photography in both Manchester and London. In 1969, one year after this photograph was taken, Bohm had a solo exhibition at the Institute of Contemporary Art, London – a rare feat at the time given that photography was viewed as a lower artistic form. In 1971, in the wake of the exhibition's popularity, Bohm went on to co-found (with Sue Davies) the Photographers' Gallery, the first public exhibition space in the United Kingdom dedicated exclusively to photographic practice.

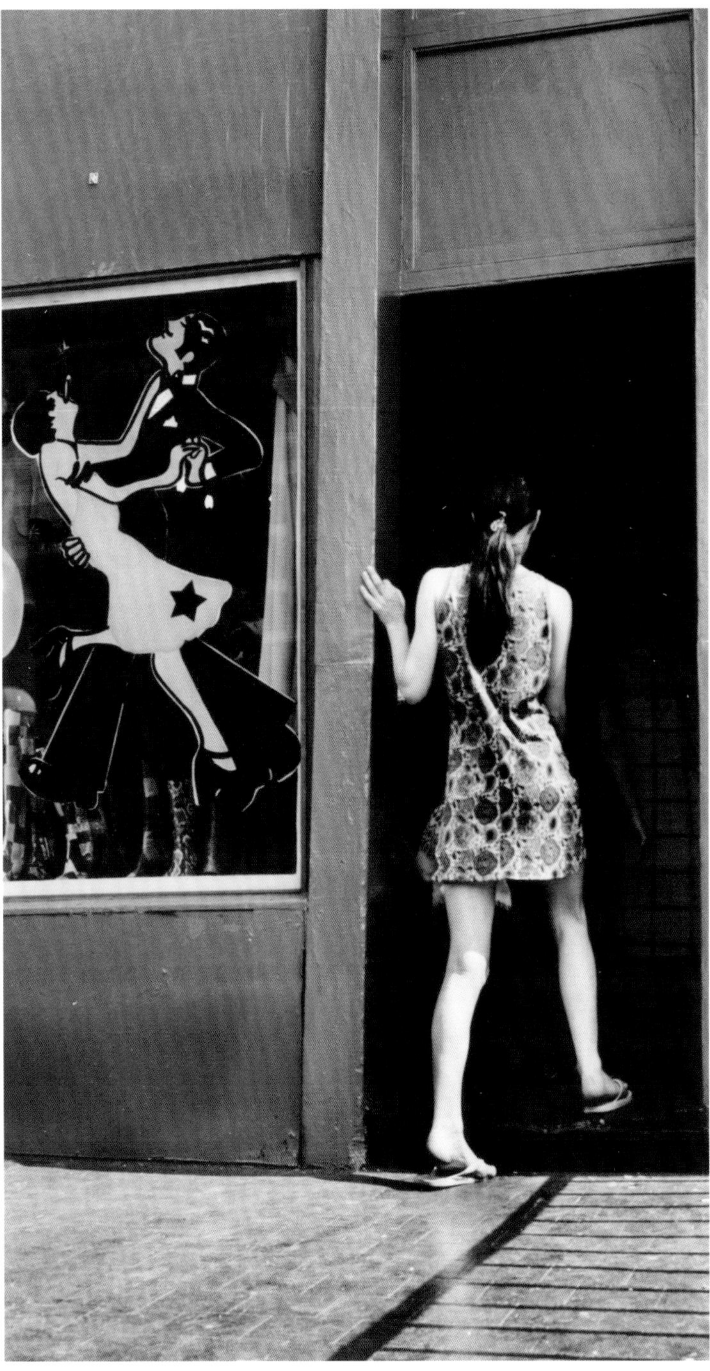

Richard Hamilton 1922–2011
Swingeing London 67 (f) 1968–9
Acrylic paint, screenprint, paper, aluminium and metalised acetate on canvas 67.3 × 85.1

Pop artist Hamilton created this work in response to the arrest of rock star Mick Jagger and Hamilton's own art dealer, Robert Fraser. These two well-known figures of Britain's 1960s nightlife scene were arrested on charges of drug possession after a police raid on the West Wittering home of the Rolling Stones' Keith Richards. Their trial took place in June, when, across the Atlantic, the self-proclaimed 'Summer of Love' was taking place in San Francisco, promoting free love, drugs and anti-consumerist hippie culture.

The title of Hamilton's work is a play on the 'swingeing' prison sentences Jagger and Fraser received from the judge. It references the *Time* magazine cover story and article, 'Swinging London', in which Fraser's eponymous gallery was featured alongside Carnaby Street fashion boutiques as one of the central spots in which the scene's movers and shakers could be spotted. The title therefore encapsulates the intensely jarring juxtaposition of the freedom of the cultural moment with this severe and shocking penal backlash.

The base image of this work, which Hamilton took from a newspaper reporting of the trial, shows the two men handcuffed and covering their eyes from the flashing lights of press photographers as they are transported from Lewes Prison to Chichester Magistrates Court. Hamilton created a number of variations on this composition, reworking the level of detail and the colouring in a manner that elevates the photographic image from mere found object to venerated motif. This particular variant includes three-dimensional aluminium elements that emphasise the handcuffs and, by extension, the intensity of the charges brought against Fraser and Jagger.

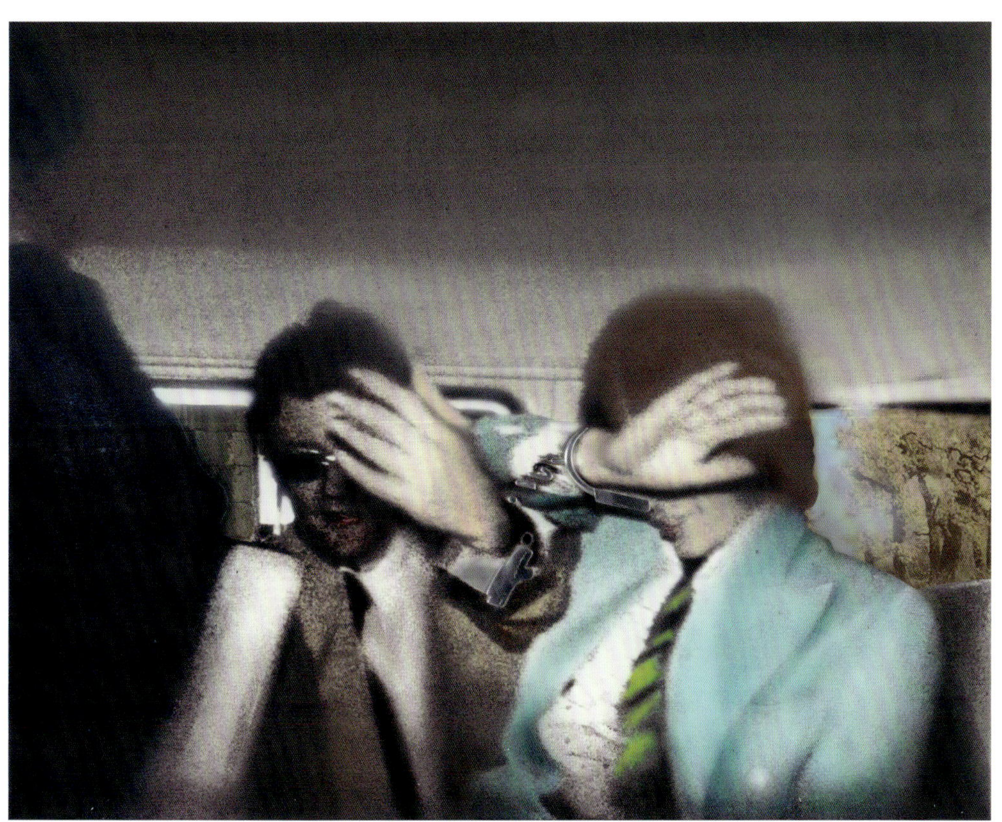

David Hockney 1937–
Mr and Mrs Clarke and Percy 1970–1
Acrylic paint on canvas 213.4 × 304.8

As part of a series of double portraits, Hockney painted the husband and wife fashion power-couple Ossie Clark and Celia Birtwell. Clark and Birtwell were married in 1969, and the work takes on the style and resonance of a traditional marriage portrait, a type of painting historically commissioned by members of wealthy families to mark an engagement or marriage. The couple's pet cat Percy and the lilies that stand proudly on the coffee table take the traditional place of a family dog (often symbolising tenderness) and meaningful floral symbolism (here, lilies symbolise fertility).

Hockney plays with this traditional form, manipulating the recognisable elements and showing the couple and their environment to be very much of their era. Flipping the expected compositional gender dynamic, Clark sits while his wife stands, hands on hips in a dominant stance. The couple stand on a thick shag rug, a relatively new interiors trend beginning to gain popularity in London with those who followed trends from America, where it had caught on in the late 1960s. Birtwell wears the Heavenly Twins dress, a design of Clark's from 1970. Although she was known for the ebullient and uniquely graphic textile designs she created for Clark's eponymous fashion line, this garment is one of the few dresses the brand created that year with fabrics that lacked her unique touch. That she wears an Ossie Clark dress, therefore, symbolises the pair's successful partnership, though the choice of the Heavenly Twins dress, with its plain fabric, demotes Birtwell's role. The dress's main defining features – its flowing shape and tighter sleeves – only celebrates the loose flowing style for which Clark was known, and which helped him to gain the moniker 'the King of King's Road' (where his boutique, Quorum, was located). This choice of dress, combined with Birtwell's lingering gaze towards the viewer, hints at a dissatisfaction plaguing the couple which the painting seeks to celebrate.

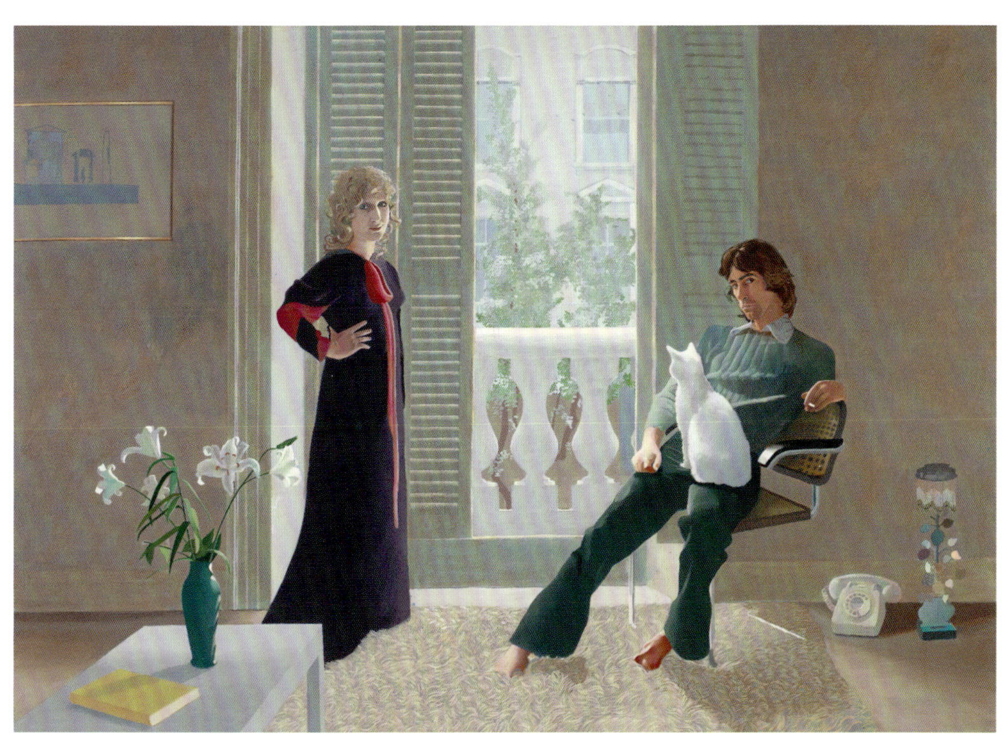

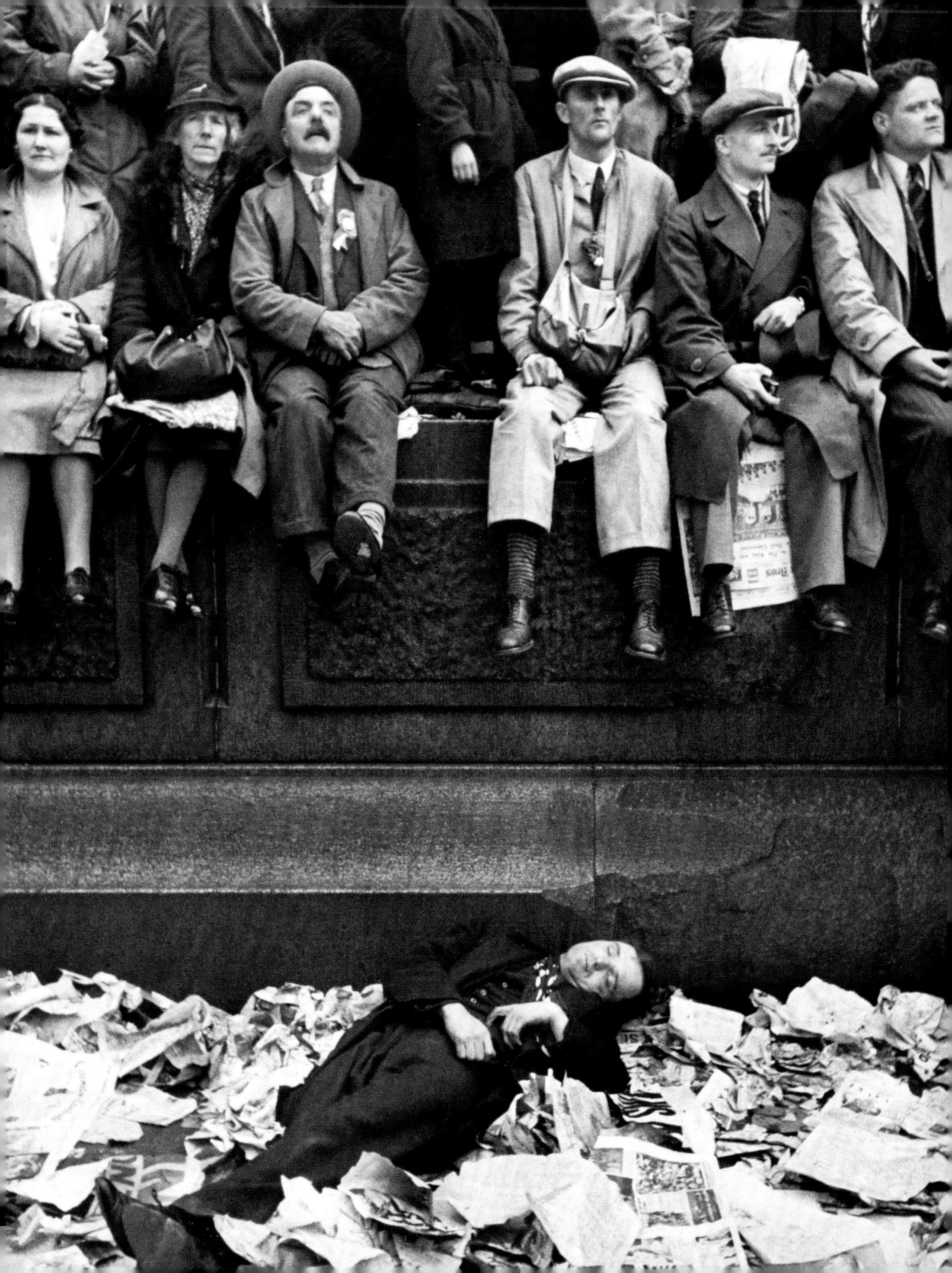

Street Style

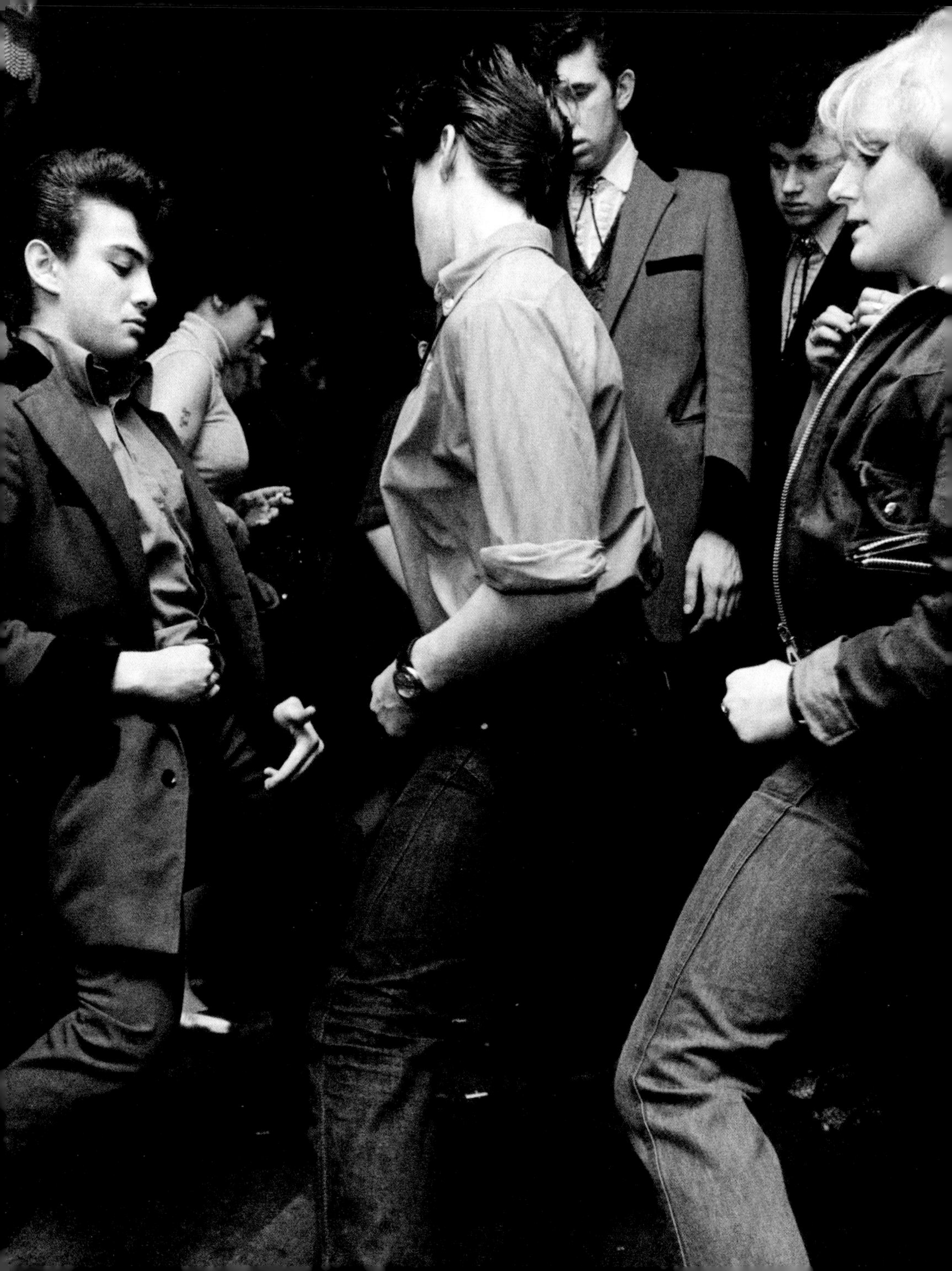

Though photographers have been taking photographs of people in public street settings ever since photographic technology was invented, the development of easily portable cameras, such as the Leica and, later, the Kodak Brownie, made the process straightforward enough that it could develop into its own distinct genre. Hungarian photographers André Kertész and Brassaï both developed advanced means of capturing outdoor photographs while living and working in Paris in the 1920s and 1930s. A great admirer of Kertész's style, Henri Cartier-Bresson combined their moveable observational aesthetic with a more personal, journalistic storytelling quality that laid the groundwork for photojournalism today. In 1947, along with a number of fellow co-founders, Cartier-Bresson established Magnum photographic agency; one of the first photojournalistic cooperatives, it shaped the field in its post-war iteration and continues to do so to this day. The ability to take photographic images for journalistic stories greatly affected the range of cultural trends and stories that could be communicated, as photographers could capture anything they came across. Fashions had always operated according to a 'top-down' structure, but now, with street photography, trends could also be created 'bottom-up': if a photograph of an individual wearing a specific style gained enough exposure, it could have as much impact as a heavily contrived fashion shoot in *Vogue*.

These photographs all document idiosyncratic trends, often belonging to subcultures whose existence and aesthetic was being shared for the first time with those who were not present or had not laid eyes on the movement personally. The images either aided in the spreading of a subcultural trend or commented – with varying degrees of admiration, journalistic distance and scepticism – upon its shape.

Chris Steele-Perkins *Adam and Eve Pub, Hackney (Teddy Boy)* 1976 (detail, see p.129) • Page 110: Henri Cartier-Bresson *Coronation of King George VI, London, 12 May 1937* 1937 (detail, see p.117)

Brassaï 1899–1984
Young Lesbian at Monocle 1932
Gelatin silver print on paper 29 × 21

In *Young Lesbian at Monocle*, Brassaï – the Hungarian photographer known for his images of Parisian nightlife in the interwar years – captures the intimate vulnerability of a young person drinking alone in a destination designed for meeting people. The sitter wears masculine clothes, including a large gold signet ring and a traditional suit and, as was in vogue for French men at the time, slicks their short hair back with a thick pomade.

Brassaï created the work in 1932 during a trip to the Montmartre lesbian nightclub Le Monocle. The name of the club referenced the trend among many young Parisian lesbians to wear a monocle along with their suits, and to slick their hair back in a distinctly masculine fashion in order to indicate their sexual identity.

Brassaï pioneered street photography, particularly photography of the night-time, and *Young Lesbian at Monocle* was published as part of his 1935 book *Paris at Night*. He walked around Paris carrying a tripod, magnesium flash powder and his camera, alongside twenty-four glass plate negatives. After identifying an interesting subject, Brassaï would talk to them, ask permission to photograph them and then set up his equipment. After the passing of time helped his subjects to become more comfortable with the equipment before them, Brassaï would take a small number of photographs of them to develop later in his makeshift kitchen darkroom. Brassaï was meticulous about befriending the communities he was interested in prior to photographing them: in his opinion, this ensured that his presence did not affect their interactions, allowing him to capture a spontaneous and authentic moment, despite the presence of his equipment and himself. As a straight man in a lesbian nightclub, however, it seems unlikely that Brassaï's presence was as inconspicuous as he intended, and it is difficult to parse the extent to which this image, as well as the others created at Le Monocle, may have featured sitters who posed slightly more intentionally than usual.

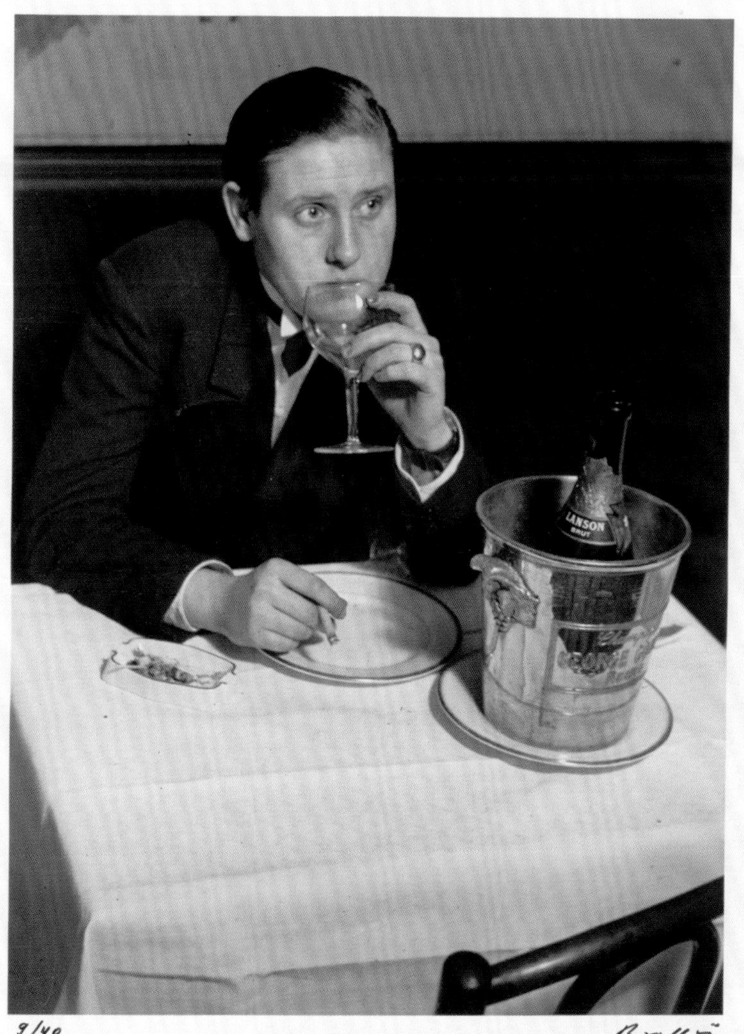

9/40

Henri Cartier-Bresson 1908–2004
Coronation of King George VI, London, 12 May 1937 1937
Gelatin silver print on paper 36 × 24

French photographer Henri Cartier-Bresson covered the coronation of George VI for the French communist publication *Ce Soir*, and his images of the event were also subsequently published in monthly Communist Party magazine *Regards*. Given his own and the publication's political leaning, Cartier-Bresson's photograph concentrates on the people in attendance on the street, rather than those invited to the official indoor ceremony.

Throughout the image, hats (and who is and is not wearing them) act as an interesting marker of class, propriety and the start of real social change. The notion that women should cover their heads at varying times or stages of their lives has featured in all three Abrahamic religions for thousands of years. In Christian Britain, this translated into the practice of women wearing structured hats when out in public. Over time, this became separated from its religious origin and thought of as an issue of propriety and indicating oneself to be a 'proper' woman. As women's roles in society began to shift after the First World War, so too did their general adherence to wearing hats at all times, and forgoing a hat started to be seen by some women as a sign of emancipation or participation in modern life. Many of the men in the photo are wearing flat caps, a style initially created in the Elizabethan era, when Parliament passed a law that all non-noblemen above the age of six must wear woollen caps on Sundays and all other national public holidays. Although the law was repealed less than thirty years after its passing, the woollen flat cap persisted, as did its association with the working classes.

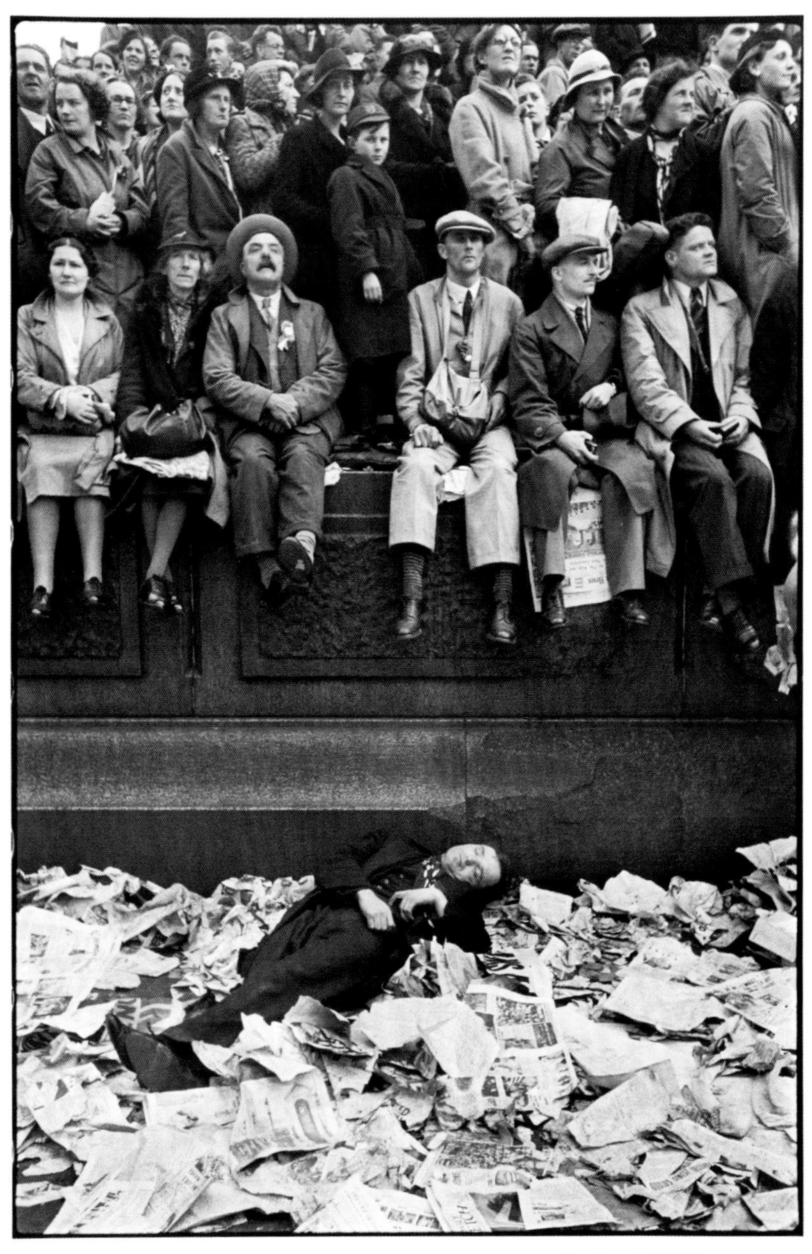

Henri Cartier-Bresson

Neil Kenlock 1950–
The Bailey Sisters in Clapham c.1970
Gelatin silver print on paper 38.4 × 25.3

In this photograph, three sisters stand next to each other, posing on a Clapham doorstep. All three women are wearing fashionable contemporary minidresses; all three are Black and also sport hairstyles free from any chemical relaxing agents or heat treatments. For hundreds of years in the West, many Black people were told (both explicitly and implicitly) that the texture of their hair was not appropriate, given that it behaved differently to that of white people. This led to the development of a variety of methods and styles that could manipulate Black people's hair so that it more closely resembled the Caucasian norm. These methods were time-consuming, often expensive and sometimes damaging to both the hair and scalp.

In the 1960s, a new trend arose for so-called 'natural' hairstyles. Black people began to wear their hair intentionally untreated, often in afros or braids. This move to re-explore and celebrate the natural beauty of Black hair initially grew in popularity from the Black Power movement in the United States and the British Black Panther movement. In 1970, around the time this photograph was taken, the afro hairstyle these women wear was heavily associated with professor and activist Angela Davis, who was on the run from the police and the FBI in the United States due to her relationship with the Soledad Brothers, three prison inmates who were charged with the murder of a prison guard. Images of Davis that highlighted her prolific afro were published widely, including on the front cover of *LIFE* magazine, accompanied by the headline 'The Making of a Fugitive'.

Originally born in Jamaica, Neil Kenlock moved to Brixton, London, as a teenager with his family and became involved in politics. At the time he took this photograph he was the official photographer of the British Black Panther movement.

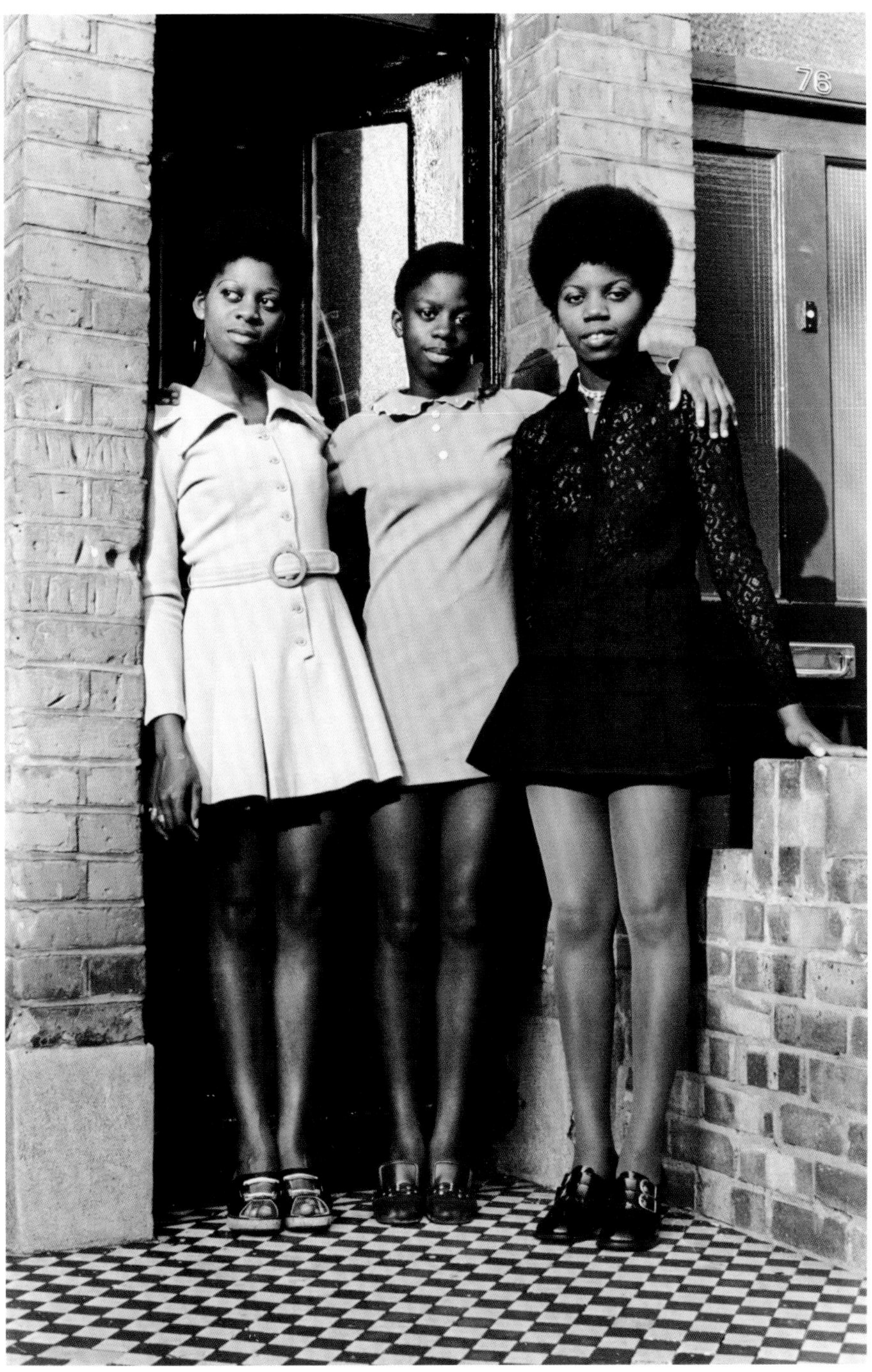
76

Sirkka-Liisa Konttinen 1948–
Lady with the Beehive (Byker) 1971
Gelatin silver print on paper 32.5 × 32.3

Finnish photographer Sirkka-Liisa Konttinen lived in the Byker neighbourhood of Newcastle-upon-Tyne in the late 1960s and early 1970s, photographing its residents. Here, a young woman sits for her portrait, wearing a shearling teddy-bear coat and sporting a beehive hairstyle created by teasing and back-brushing the hair to give it structure and volume. The hair is then pinned at the back, creating the appearance of great height and shape.

Chicago-based hairstylist Margaret Vinci Heldt created the beehive style in 1960, having been inspired by the shape of a fez hat while working at a photoshoot for the trade publication *Modern Beauty Salon*. The look was immediately popular, spreading rapidly throughout much of the West, and was worn by many major celebrities of the 1960s, including Brigitte Bardot, Audrey Hepburn and Aretha Franklin. The style did not just hold celebrity appeal; with its copious layers of hairspray, setting cream and the volume of the combed hair, the beehive endured for longer than most of the fashionable hairstyles that had preceded it, and was adopted as another symbol of the 1960s' celebration of liberated women. By the time Konttinen took this photograph, the beehive was no longer particularly cutting-edge, and the titling of this work may serve to point out how the subject's stylistic choices are somewhat behind the times.

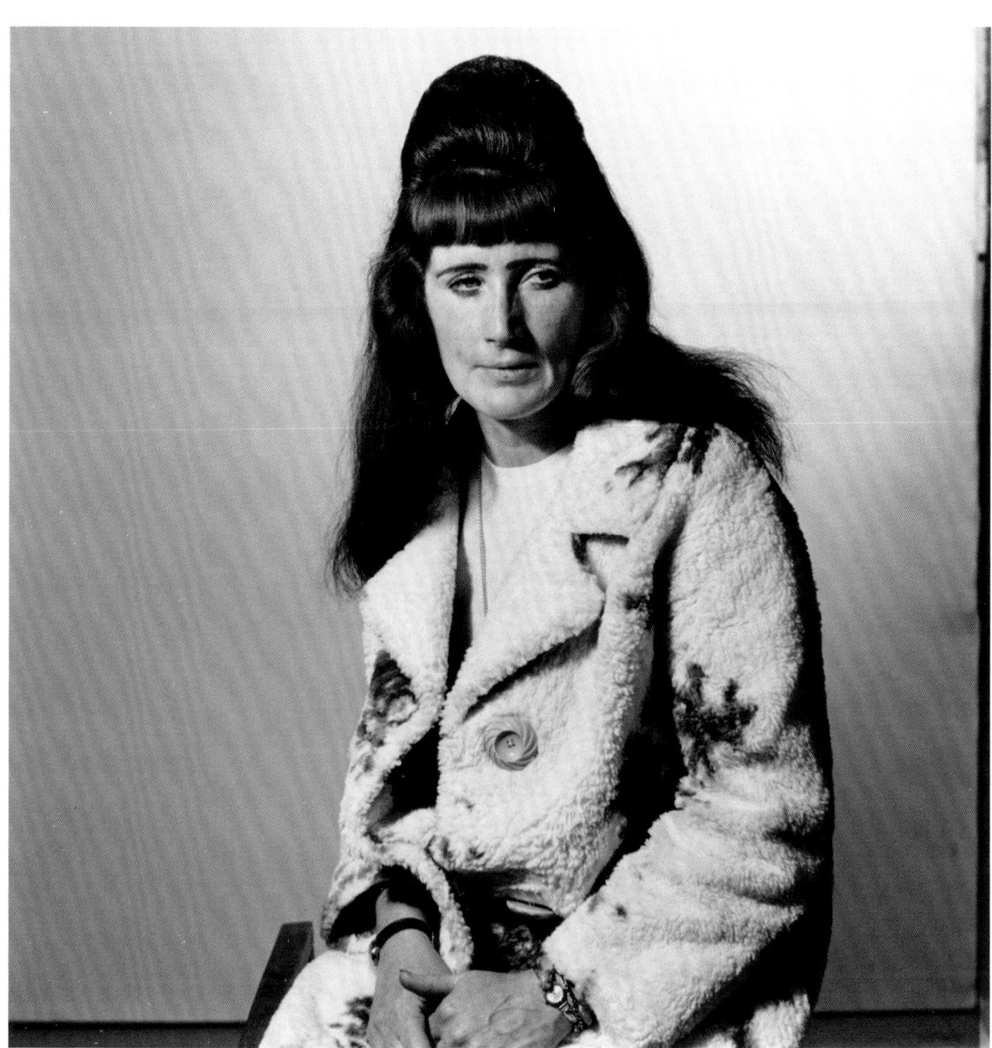

Al Vandenberg 1932–2012
Untitled from the series *On a Good Day* c.1975–80
Gelatin silver print on paper 18.9 × 11.7

Al Vandenberg's photo from the series *On a Good Day* captures two young teenagers, dressed in matching outfits, standing before a brick wall. Both wear hats and wide-fit trousers that are cropped, allowing their socks, ankles and shoes to serve as more of a focus. The cuffs of their trousers are decorated with a tartan-style fabric that matches the scarves draped around their necks.

Like anarchic political statements, tartan was associated in the 1970s with the punk movement. The Sex Pistols' Johnny Rotten was known for wearing a suit made entirely of tartan; notably, he performed in one at a 1977 gig during which he called the Queen of England a 'fascist'.

Given its history in Britain, tartan was perhaps a particularly fitting pattern to don while making punk statements. Historically worn in the north of Scotland as the material of a kilt, it was officially outlawed by English Parliament in the Dress Act of 1746, which banned the wearing of tartan materials and other elements of traditional Scottish dress by men in the Scottish Highlands. This was an attempt to quell rising nationalist sympathies and calls for an independent Scotland. Though the Act was repealed after fifty years, tartan maintains the allure of something forbidden and, for many, stands for calls to break away from the imperialism of Westminster's Parliament.

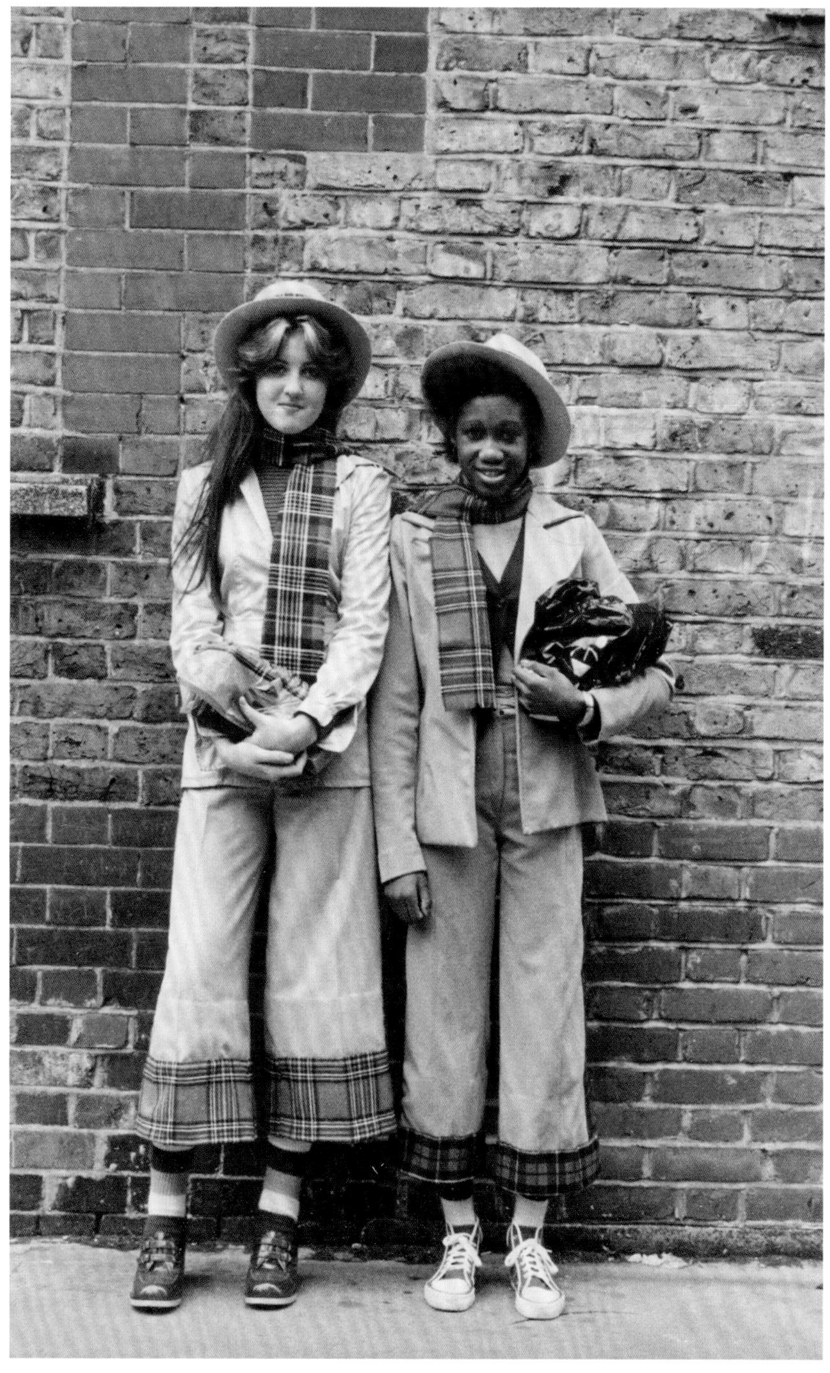

Karen Knorr and Olivier Richon 1954– and 1956–
Destroy from the *Punks* series 1976
Gelatin silver print on paper 26 × 17.8

In this collaboration between two UK-based photographers, the words 'Destroy London' emblazoned on the back of a creased leather jacket take centre stage. In 1976, the year this image was created, this provocative and borderline violent wording would have been instantly read as belonging to the punk subculture, which emerged that same year. The movement initially coalesced around Vivienne Westwood and Malcolm McLaren's SEX shop on the King's Road in London; though specialising in fetishwear, the shop also stocked a large supply of clothing with politically suggestive slogans and images.

The Sex Pistols, a band almost synonymous with the movement, formed from a group of people associated with the shop and, with their commercial success, brought the anarchic protest aesthetic to a wider public. Setting themselves distinctly apart from British musical stalwarts such as The Rolling Stones, The Sex Pistols eschewed any kind of kowtowing to the class or cultural establishment. In 1976, the group appeared live on the BBC, wearing an array of controversial clothing, including images of breasts and Nazi swastika armbands. Breaking the rules regarding appropriate language for live television, they swore and told the presenter Bill Grundy that he was a 'dirty bastard' and a 'dirty fucker'. Even though newspapers across the political spectrum throughout the UK decried the incident on their front pages the next day, the appearance resonated with disillusioned youth across the country, who adopted similar fashion choices and developed the punk movement further.

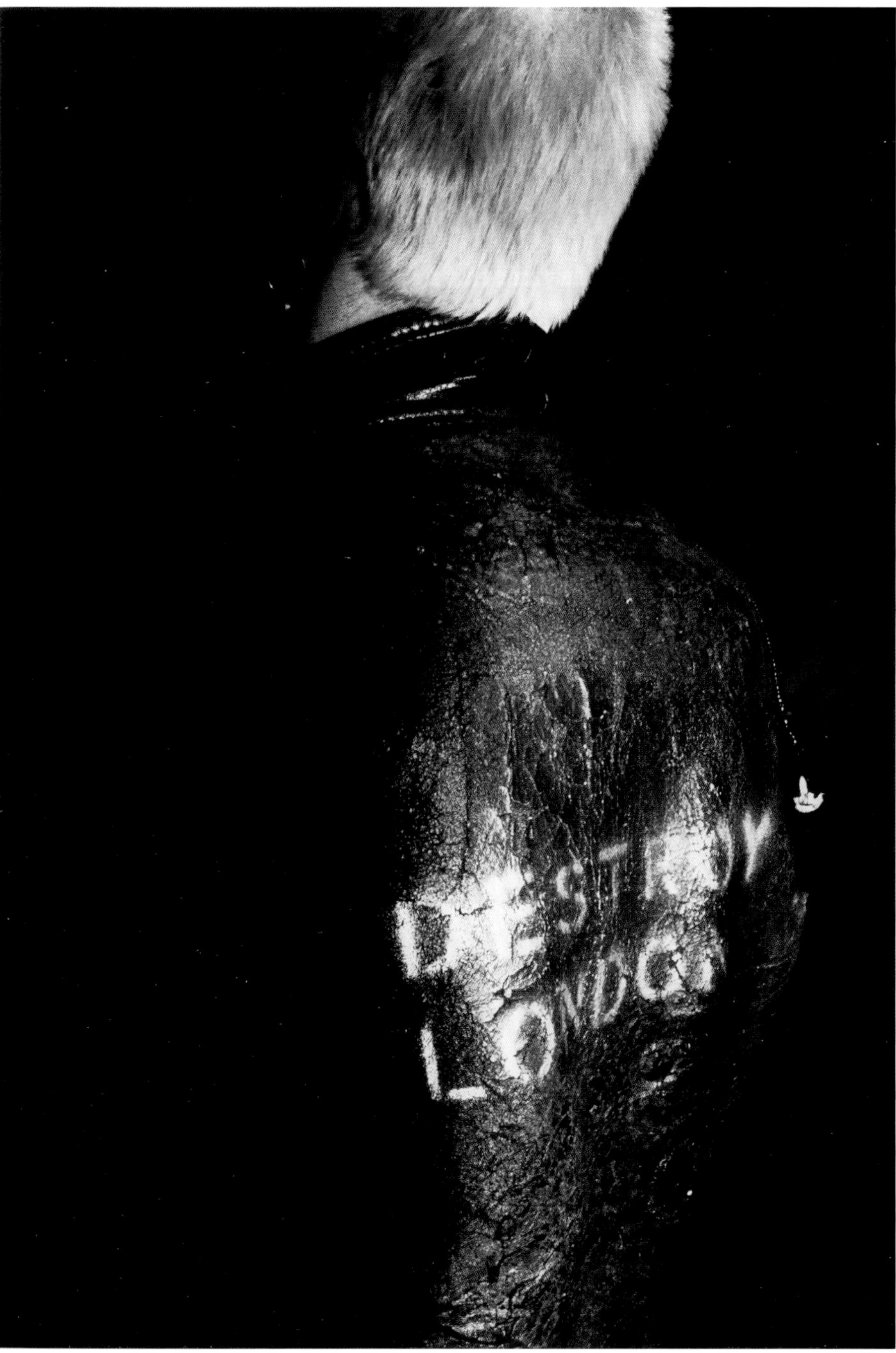

Mario de Biasi 1923–2013
London 1974
Gelatin silver print on paper 30 × 21.2

This photograph candidly documents two young people making their way through London's streets. Though the woman is dressed in a fairly plain ensemble of sleeveless turtleneck top and miniskirt, her companion's get-up is rather more unusual. His outfit of wing-collared shirt, striped tie, longline blazer and top hat is rather less run-of-the-mill than his nonchalant pose might suggest. In his extravagant pastiche of the interwar fashions of the upper classes and silver screen-era Hollywood, he firmly identifies himself as a member of the glam rock subculture. Emerging in the late 1960s and early 1970s, glam rock merged references to the glamorous parties of an earlier age with a reverence for contemporary rock stars, whose performances were broadcast live across Britain every Friday night on television show *Top of the Pops*.

Glam rockers did not merely look up to these rock gods, but emulated their performative theatricality. More than their glamorous looks, it was their sense of exaggeration, excess and fantasy that served as the true marker of the movement. In addition, there was a decidedly non-heterosexual edge to the movement and its aesthetic presentations. Figures like Alice Cooper and David Bowie inhabited a space in which their sexuality was deliberately ambivalent. Walking together arm in arm dressed as they are, the subjects of De Biasi's image provoke the viewer, defying them to assume any specific sexual identity on the couple's behalf.

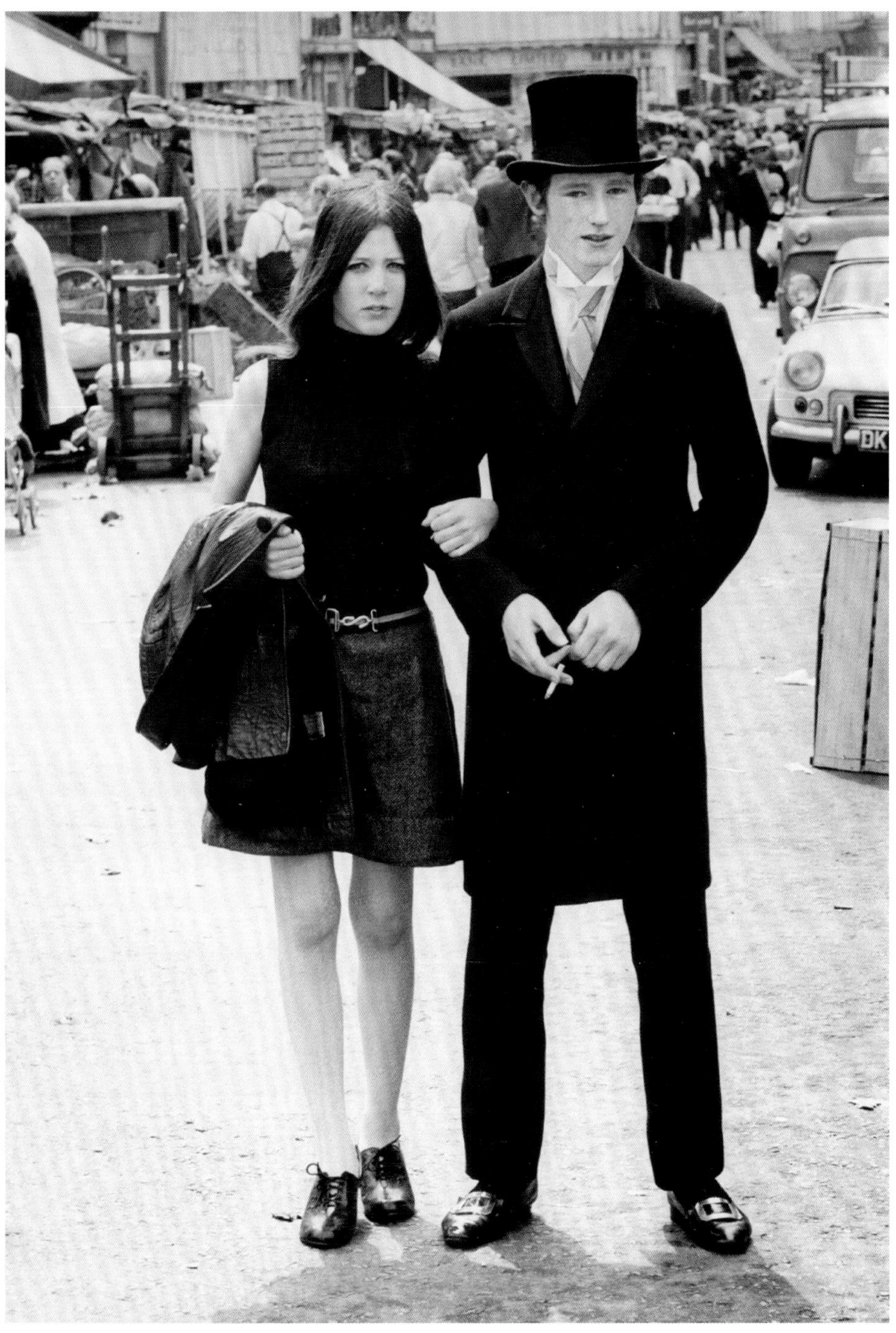

Chris Steele-Perkins 1944–
Adam and Eve Pub, Hackney (Teddy Boy) 1976
Gelatin silver print 21.6 × 30.5

Steele-Perkins's photograph captures the rebellious spirit of a cultural phenomenon that took 1970s British youth by storm: the 'Teddy boy'. Teddy boys could be identified by their unique clothing style: they wore 'creeper' platformed shoes with 'skinny' trousers that tapered at the bottom, and often finished this off with a gelled roll of hair atop their head.

The photograph captures the specific mood and look of the culture, but also offers a glimpse into the emergence of a new stage in life. In the aftermath of the Second World War – during which many families had sent their children away to protect their lives – the gulf between those returning children and their parents was far more noticeable than it had been before. This led to the recognition of a phase of life younger than adulthood and older than childhood: the teenager. The Teddy boy subculture was among the first to spread exclusively among this newly acknowledged demographic and images of them carry a special weight.

Steele-Perkins himself was a fan of the Teddy boy culture, and even went out to buy his own Teddy boy clothes, intending to start dressing in a way that would publicly identify him as a member of the subculture. His father, however, took such umbrage with the idea that he gathered all of his son's new wardrobe and burned the garments in a show of protest. Steele-Perkins's fraught but aspirational history with Teddy boys allows the image to be read as a later, post-teenaged attempt at engaging with a culture that had once been declared off-limits to him. The photograph might resonate with viewers whose wish to become a part of this world had been similarly quashed.

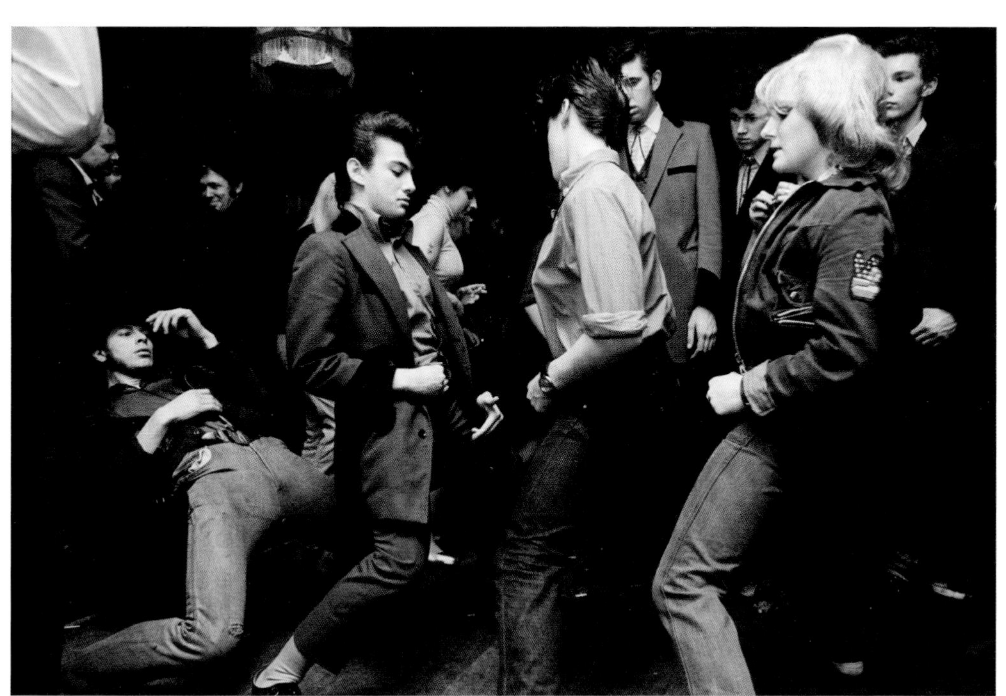

Martine Franck 1938–2012
Greenwich, London 1977
Gelatin silver print on paper 36 × 24.2

Greenwich, London focuses on the faces and clothing of young children standing behind a barrier. Though taken on the day of Elizabeth II's 1977 Silver Jubilee, Franck focuses on the crowd rather than the procession and accompanying festivities themselves. The British flag, the Union Jack, features heavily, particularly upon the card top hats the two children in the work are wearing. Topped with the official Silver Jubilee photograph of the Queen, the hats suggest an enthusiasm their faces and body language do not.

The choice of the top hat as a form of celebratory headgear references the sustained presence of top hats in certain parts of British society. Though the hat's prominence declined significantly over the course of the twentieth century, it still featured among the formal dress codes for roles such as King's College choristers, certain senior Bank of England roles and dressage riders. In 1977, these were all positions typically inhabited by the members of Britain's upper class. The hat here, by contrast, is made of cardboard and somewhat kitsch. Worn by an unenthusiastic child, who presumably does not belong to the upper echelons of privileged society, it offers a potentially republican challenge to the more conventional shots of the Jubilee that would have been published in newspapers around the world the next day.

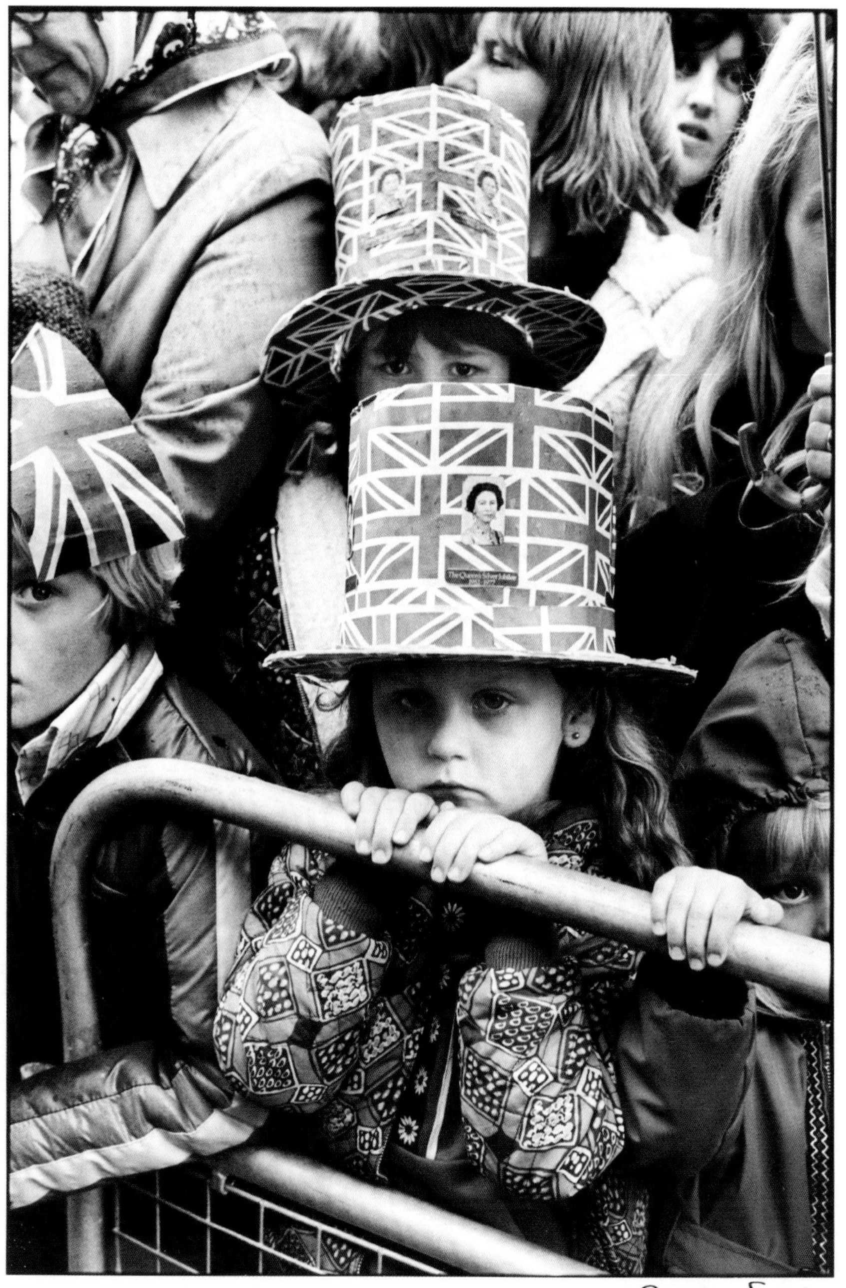

Martine Franck

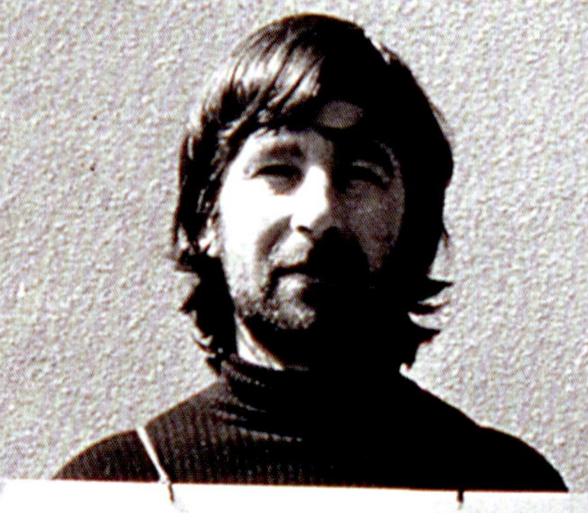
I'M A
REAL
ARTIST

Fashioning the Self

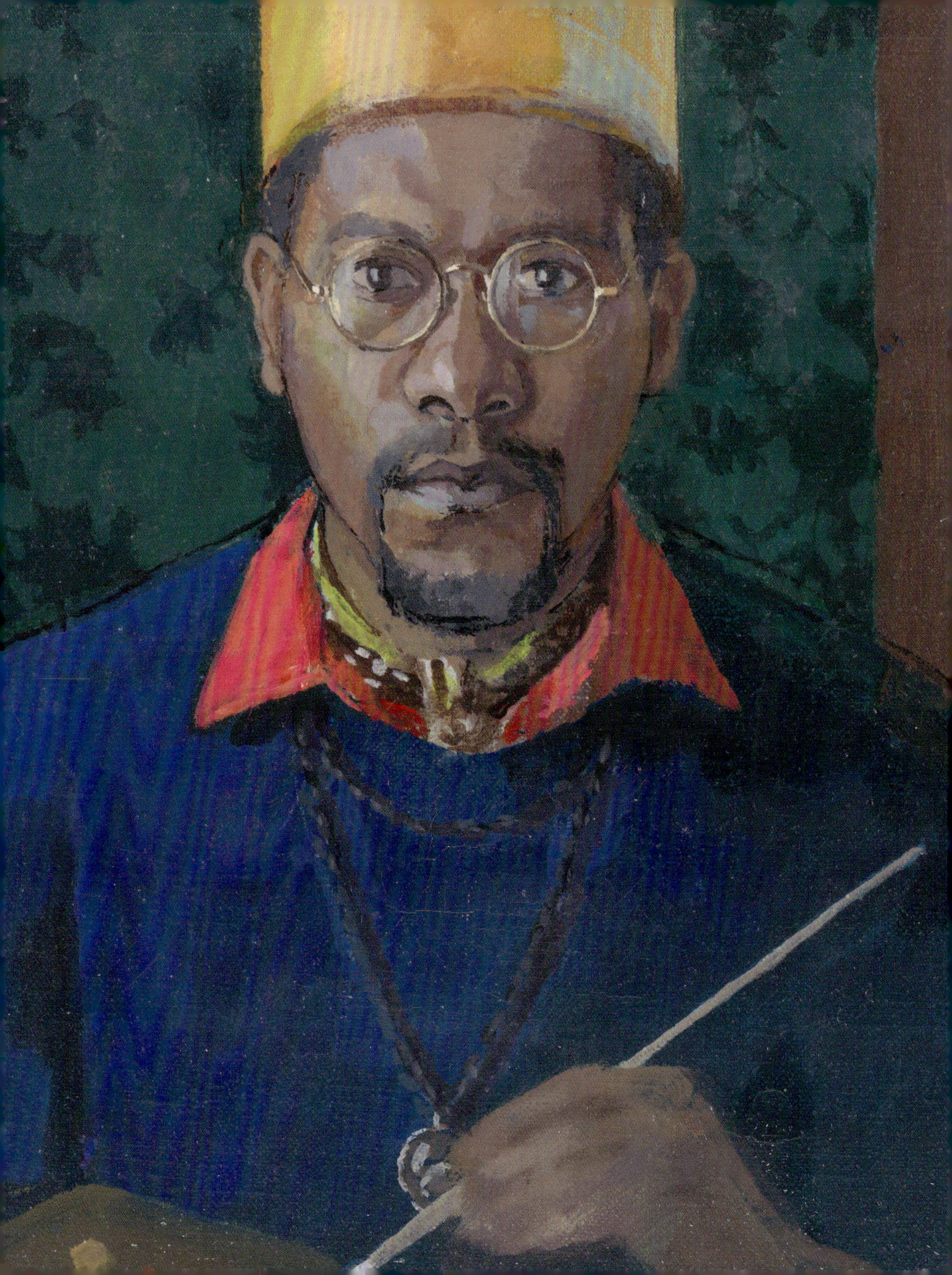

For the artist, the presentation of the self both in everyday life and in self-portraiture can serve as a key mode of signalling their own prejudices and influences – as well as the fellow artists with whom they wish to be associated. In the West in the late nineteenth century, biographies became a particularly popular genre of book; subsequently, artists themselves became objects of fascination and discussion independently of their artistic output. They began to face increasing scrutiny of their lifestyle and dress, in a way that could greatly affect their professional success. Dress, examined by artist and viewer alike, became a key element of the artistic persona in this era.

In nineteenth-century France, the beret was an inexpensive hat traditionally worn by agricultural workers. During industrialisation, many of these workers moved to cities to work in newly-constructed factories, bringing their berets with them. Consequently, the beret came to signify that the wearer belonged to the working class. After prominent French artists including Paul Cézanne and Claude Monet started wearing berets in their own official self-portraits, artists in other countries such as the United States and Britain – who saw Paris as more artistically sophisticated – began to adopt the beret to show their affinity for French aesthetics.

In the early twentieth century, not wearing a beret could be as much of a statement as wearing one, as it signalled how French-facing an artist was. Italian futurist Giacomo Balla proudly forwent the beret, instead donning check suits and ties made of untraditional fabrics, including wood, plastic and cardboard. He stuck lightbulbs to his ties, turning them on at moments of conversation he felt to be particularly 'electrifying.'

The pages that follow analyse the sartorial presentations of artists from the twentieth and twenty-first centuries. The choice of clothing in each image, as well its presentation, composition and referents, allows us to situate the artist more precisely within their oeuvre.

Paul Dash *Self-Portrait* 1979 (detail, see p.149). • Page 132: Keith Arnatt *Trouser-Word Piece* 1972 (detail, see p.143)

Gwen John 1876–1939
Self-Portrait 1902
Oil paint on canvas 44.8 × 34.9

The ultimate symbol of women's emancipation in late nineteenth- and early twentieth-century England and America was the New Woman. She was educated, independent and seen as somewhat masculine in a manner new to women in the public eye. Politically, the latter half of the nineteenth century had seen great change in the area of women's rights. In England, most notably, the 1857 Matrimonial Causes Act and the 1870 Married Women's Property Act changed the ability of women to live independently of men. Gwen John studied at the Slade School of Art, where female students, rather radically, made up two thirds of the student population. While John was studying there, from 1895 to 1898, debate raged regarding the rights of female students around the country after the University of Cambridge formally voted to deny women the right to a degree, even if they proved able to complete all coursework and pass all examinations. Women wishing to access such a degree were portrayed in the media as New Women, with puffed sleeves, button-down shirts with cinched waists, a necktie or bow and their hair tied in a bun.

In her 1902 *Self-Portrait*, John depicts herself in just such a manner. Her bold red shirt comes in at the waist and her hairstyle is also part of the visual language of the New Woman identity. As if to erase any doubt about her identification with this movement and new trend in women's lives, John wears a black ribbon around her neck, adorned with a miniature portrait, adding an artistic twist to the New Woman trend. John's self-portrait, then, shows her explicitly identifying as a New Woman, ready to explore brand new opportunities only just opened to women.

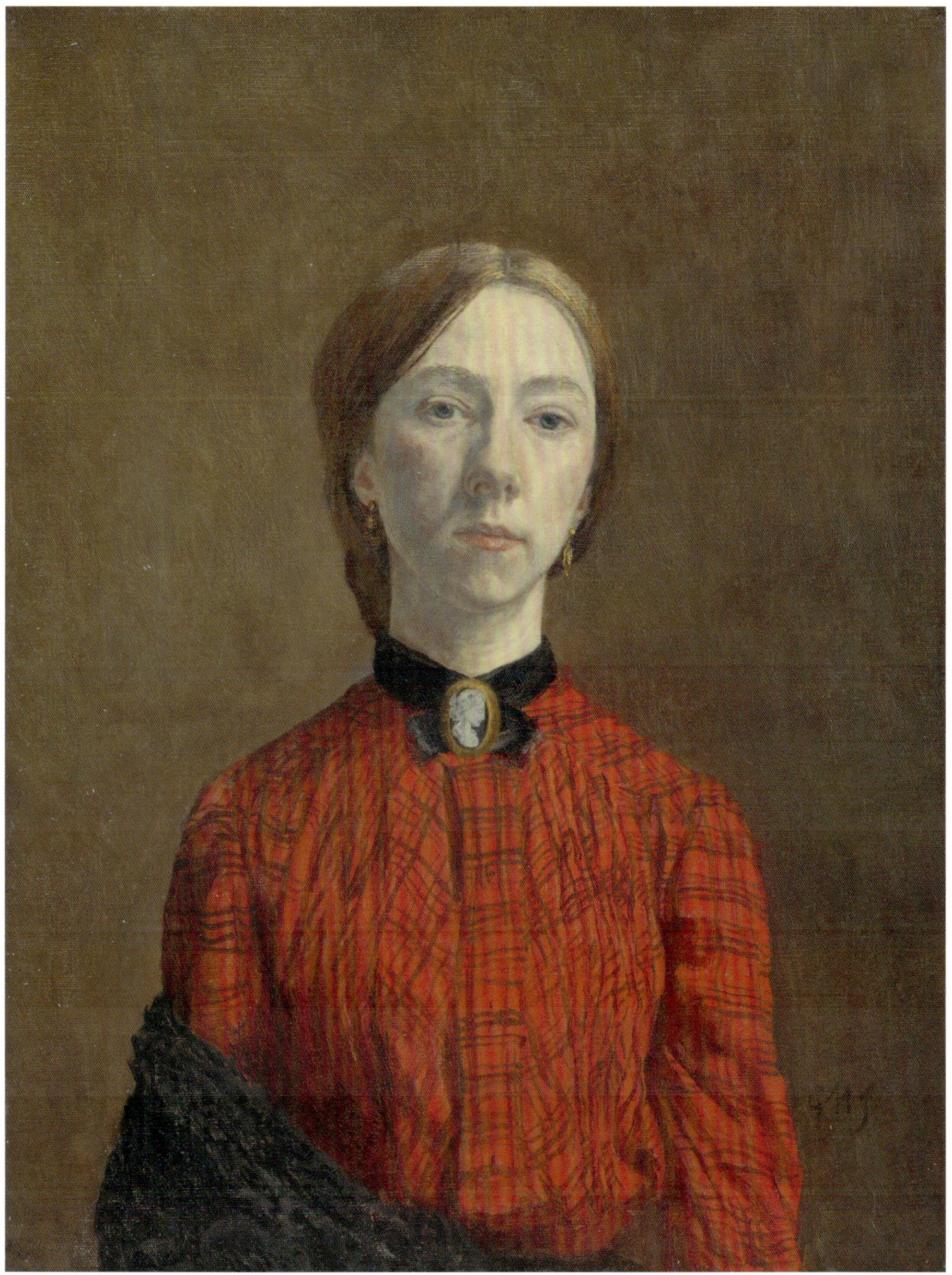

Vanessa Bell 1879–1961
Self-Portrait 1915
Oil paint on canvas 63.8 × 45.9

Hailing from an artistic family, Vanessa Bell's talents were recognised at a young age. As soon as she was able, she applied to and was accepted to study at the Royal Academy. After her graduation and the death of her father, she moved to a house in Gordon Square, Bloomsbury, with her siblings, where a circle of intellectuals, dubbed the Bloomsbury Group, grew up around them. Bell created this painting while a member of the Omega Workshops, a commercial endeavour set up by her and other members of the Bloomsbury Group to create accessible domestic design for the public that reflected the Bloomsbury Group's radical aesthetics.

Before a multicoloured, unrecognisable backdrop, Bell looks out from her *Self-Portrait*. She wears a dress that plunges rather low on her chest, in a matter-of-fact manner that does not sexualise her. A pink trim frames her neckline and falls down the middle of her dress, emphasising the navy tie that secures the empire-line cut of her dress. In April 1915, Bell proposed adding dress design to the already extensive catalogue of Omega Workshops production and, under her direction, the workshop subsequently expanded its offerings to clothing.

Tasked with styling the publicity images of her clothing designs, Bell herself modelled the dresses, alongside fellow workshop members Nina Hamnett and Winifred Gill. Omega's manager, Charles Robinson, vetoed the image of Bell wearing Omega clothing, however, and requested that the image be reshot with a more petite employee of the workshop, Joy Brown. Bell's choice of a similar dress in her *Self-Portrait* of the same year may be interpreted as a form of resistance to the workshop manager, a reimagining of the publicity photo she was barred from featuring in.

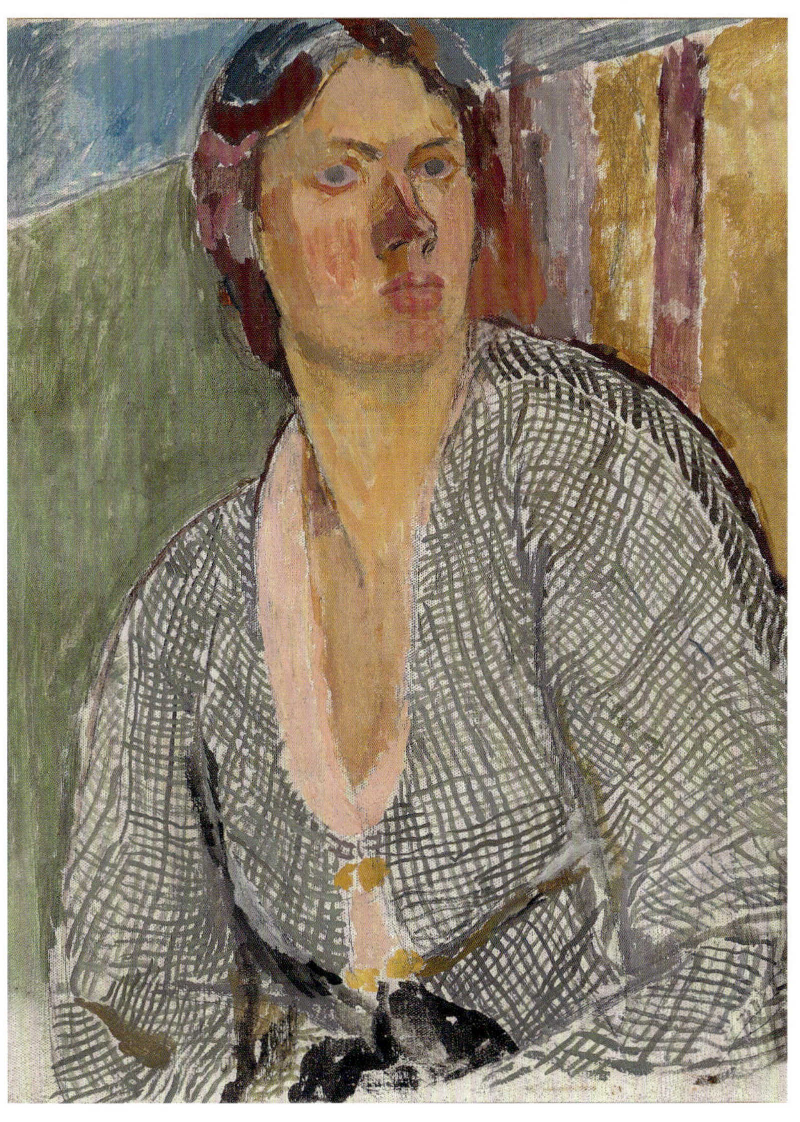

Sylvia Sleigh 1916–2010
The Bride (Lawrence Alloway) 1949
Oil paint on canvas 61 × 50.8

Welsh artist Sylvia Sleigh painted this work as a visual love letter to her partner Lawrence Alloway. After they met at art history evening classes when she was twenty-seven and he was seventeen, they entered into a friendship that later turned into a romance. Although Sleigh was still married to her first husband at the time, the painting was created during a trip she and Alloway took to Italy, which they referred to as their 'honeymoon'. The portrait provocatively refers to Alloway as 'the bride' in their relationship, referring to his habit of dressing as a woman, usually in the form of his alter ego 'Hetty Remington', as shown here.

Inspired by Renaissance and Rococo painting, Alloway's outfit and pose are somewhat reminiscent of clothes Elizabeth I of England wears in surviving royal portraits. In the famous *Armada Portrait* 1588, beads adorn the monarch's hair and multiple strands of pearls hang from the ruff around her neck. In the twentieth century, Coco Chanel had also popularised wearing layered strands of pearls as a modern fashion statement. Pearls had a newly accessible price point in the early twentieth century, thanks to Japanese company Mikimoto, who mastered the ability to artificially culture and farm perfectly spherical pearls for the market. In *The Bride*, Alloway's outfit references female fashion icons both old and new, blending them together to form a thoroughly contemporary portrait of a distinctly modern partnership.

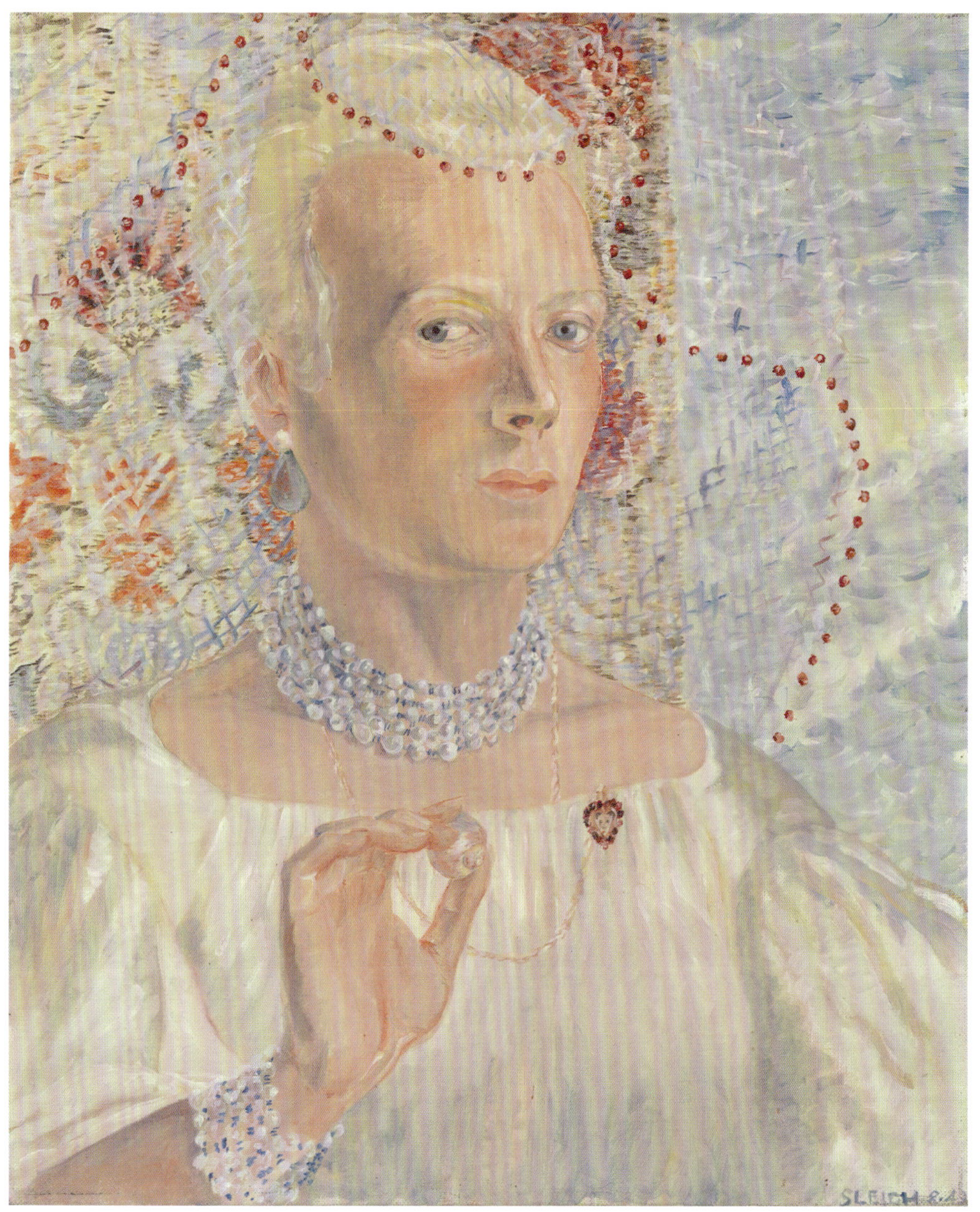
SLEIGH

Keith Arnatt 1930–2008
Trouser-Word Piece 1972, 1989 version
Gelatin silver prints on paper 100.5 × 100.5 each

In *Trouser-Word Piece*, Keith Arnatt engages conceptually with the notion of what it might mean to be an artist and to present yourself as one. In place of any of the visual posturing that has been used throughout the ages to signify the occupation of artist, Arnatt uses a simple wearable sign in sans-serif lettering. He wears otherwise plain black clothing, and stands before a simple and unidentifiable background. The image is printed in black and white, further simplifying the aesthetic elements of Arnatt's self-portrait as artist – that is, the only thing within the work that links him to artistic sentiment is his sign. The image is printed next to an extract from the work of philosopher J.L. Austin, *Sense and Sensibilia*, in which he talks about the way the word 'real' functions. In the extract, Austin posits that 'with "real" ... it is the *negative* use that wears the trousers. That is, a definite sense attaches to the assertion that something is real, a real such-and-such, only in the light of a specific way in which it might be, or might have been, *not* real.'

After studying at the Oxford School of Art and the Royal Academy of Art, Arnatt developed a robust conceptual art practice, often using his body in relation to the environment around him. Arnatt regularly used performance, which he documented using photography and film, as a key element of his artistic work. Arnatt initially published *Trouser-Word Piece* in the catalogue for the Hayward Gallery's 1972 exhibition *The New Art*, but later reprinted the work as a larger stand-alone piece in 1989.

Keith Arnatt

TROUSER – WORD PIECE

'It is usually thought, and I dare say usually rightly thought, that what one might call the affirmative use of a term is basic - that, to understand 'x', we need to know what it is to be x, or to be an x, and that knowing this apprises us of what it is **not** to be x, not to be an x. But with 'real' . . . . it is the **negative** use that wears the trousers. That is, a definite sense attaches to the assertion that something is real, a real such-and-such, only in the light of a specific way in which it might be, or might have been, **not** real. 'A real duck' differs from the simple 'a duck' only in that it is used to exclude various ways of being not a real duck - but a dummy, a toy, a picture, a decoy, &c.; and moreover I don't know **just** how to take the assertion that it's a real duck unless I know **just** what, on that particular occasion, the speaker had it in mind to exclude . . . . (The) function of 'real' is not to contribute positively to the characterisation of anything, but to exclude possible ways of being **not** real - and these ways are both numerous for particular kinds of things, and liable to be quite different for things of different kinds. It is this identity of general function combined with immense diversity in specific applications which gives to the word 'real' the, at first sight, baffling feature of having neither one single 'meaning,' nor yet ambiguity, a number of different meanings.'

John Austin, 'Sense and Sensibilia.'

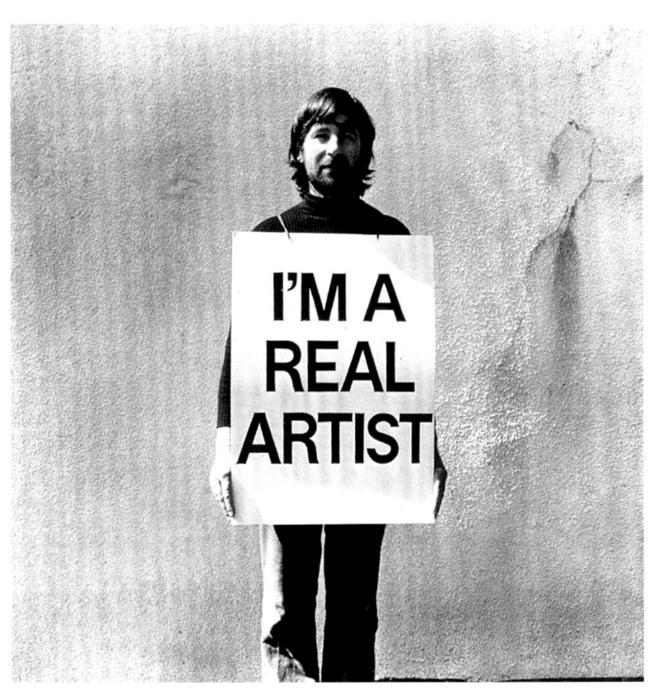

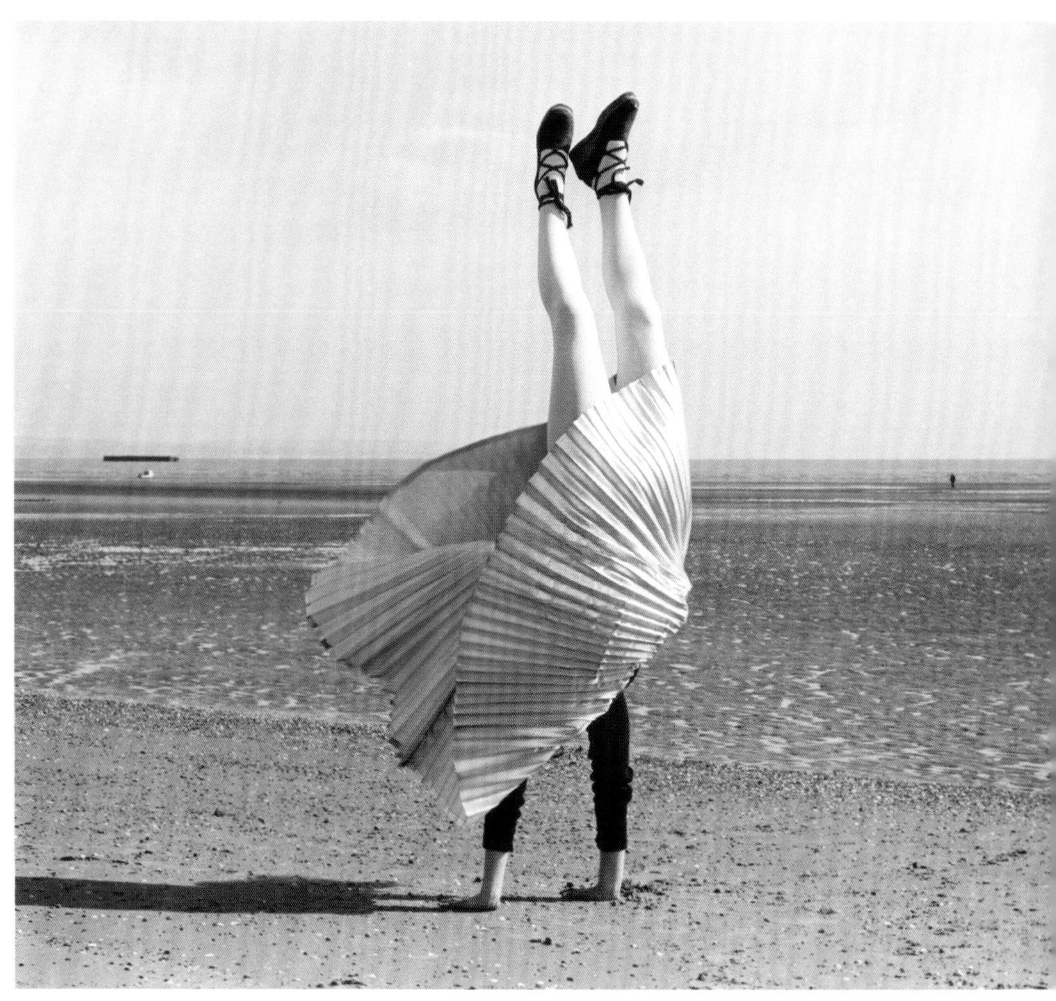

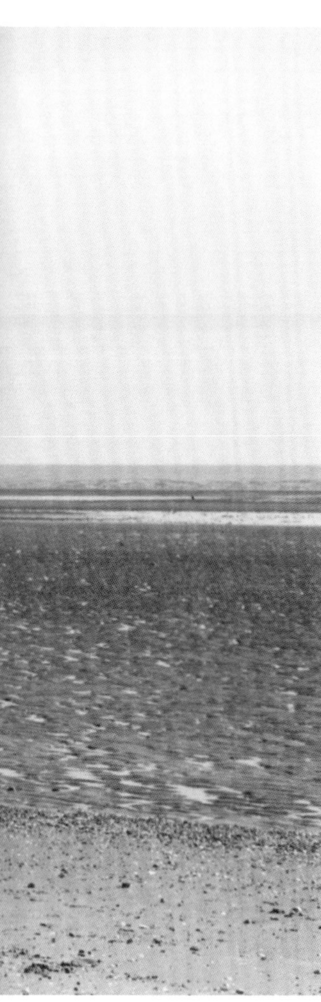

Rose Finn-Kelcey 1945–2014
The Restless Image: a discrepancy between the felt position and the seen position 1975
Gelatin silver print on paper mounted on board 66.4 × 101.4

Finn-Kelcey created this as an homage to an image of her mother doing handstands on the beach, which she found particularly meaningful. The first part of the work's title, 'the restless image', takes its name from sociologist René König's book *The Restless Image: A Sociology of Fashion*, in which König argues for a conception of fashion as historical, sociological, but also psychological, based in an understanding of class, circumstance and morality, as well as cyclical aesthetic trends. The second part of the work's title, 'a discrepancy between the felt position and the seen position', ties into a major theme of Finn-Kelcey's work – the inconsistency between how something might be observed and how it actually is for the person experiencing it. While a handstand on sand may seem like a carefree and fun-filled gesture, it is, perhaps, a rather strange means of constructing a self-portrait. The movement obscures Finn-Kelcey's entire torso and head and, in spite of the relative intimacy of her bared legs, the viewer comes away without any concrete ability to identify the artist should they ever encounter her. Perhaps this obscurity, then, is deliberate – the deception hinted at in the title.

Although espadrilles have been worn in Catalonia for thousands of years, they gained specific popularity outside of the region in the twentieth century among artists who wished to mimic espadrille-wearer Salvador Dalí. Later, in 1970, Yves Saint Laurent and shoe company Castañer collaborated and created the wedged espadrille, igniting the 1970s craze for the style of shoe Finn-Kelcey wears in this image. These two potential reference points further compound the unknowability of Finn-Kelcey's gesture: is she modelling herself as a surrealist or a high fashion follower?

Cindy Sherman 1954–
Untitled Film Still #17 1978
Gelatin silver print on paper 74.5 × 95

American artist Cindy Sherman made a series of sixty-nine black-and-white photographs between 1977 and 1980 as part of her *Untitled Film Stills* series. The type of photographic film stills Sherman references here are not, in fact, stills from a film but rather photographs created to evoke the atmosphere of the film and used in its promotion. Throughout the series, Sherman acts out various types of female cliché that women's roles fell into in the early days of cinema. Sherman collected vintage clothing for this purpose and saw the choice of clothing as a deliberate part of the work, adding to the tense atmosphere. In *Untitled Film Still #17*, she presents herself to the camera in a bobbed wig covered by a scarf; she wears a floral cardigan and a pussy-bow blouse, and her eyes are rimmed with black kohl. She has commented that 'the clothes make [the characters in the series] seem a certain way, but then you look at their expression, however slight it may be, and wonder if maybe "they" are not what the clothes are communicating.'

Like the women in her film stills, who become more distant and impenetrable as the viewer notices more details, Sherman herself demonstrates her own fundamentally amorphous nature. Her face features throughout her work, in so many different forms and manners, that her own character becomes unknowable; the series acts as a form of anti-self-portrait, taunting the viewer of the photograph, who is desperate for a morsel of reality and veracity that will not come.

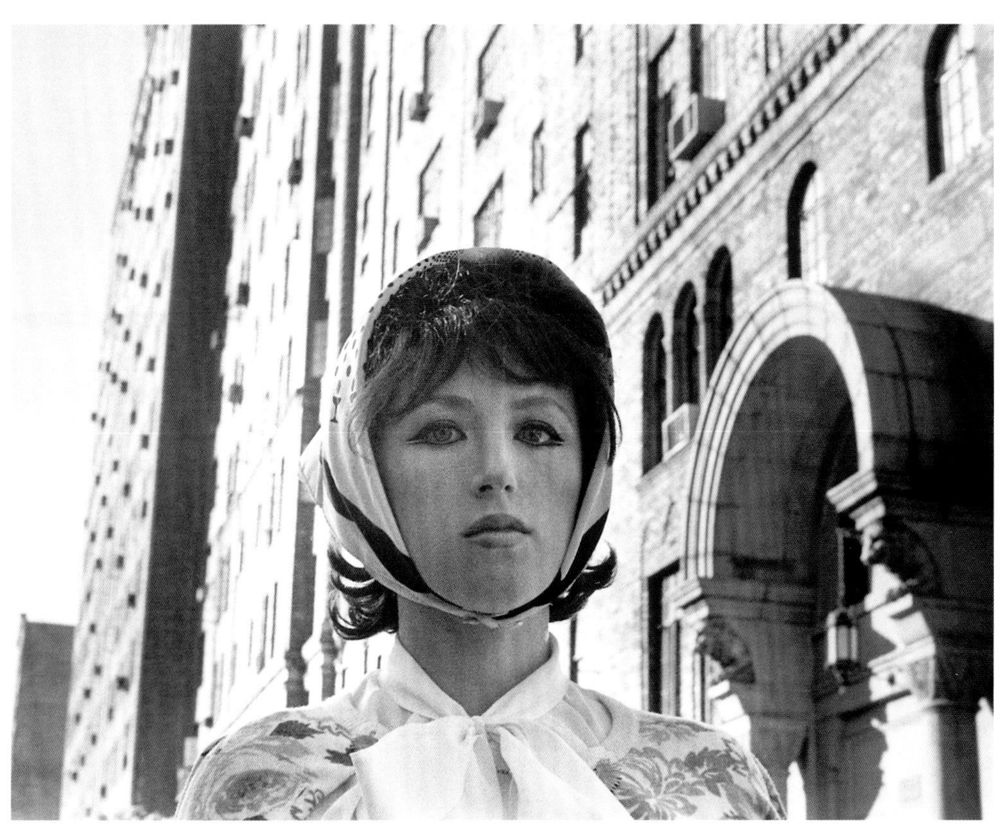

Paul Dash 1946–
Self-Portrait 1979
Oil paint on canvas 32.9 × 25.2

Dash's painting makes reference to the tradition of self-portraits in which the artist is often shown carrying a paint palette and wearing a stylised hat, such as those by Édouard Manet (*Self Portrait with Palette* 1878–9) and Paul Gauguin (*Self Portrait with Palette* c.1894). Compositionally, Dash depicts himself in a conventional style that identifies him squarely as a modern Western painter. In colour and sartorial choices, however, Dash explores a mode of depiction that points towards his lived experience as a Black man born in Barbados, now living in London. Dash stands before a slice of green wallpaper that serves as a contrasting backdrop to the deep colours of his skin. Complementary brown tones sandwich this piece of wallpaper – and, by extension, Dash himself – between two panels that highlight Dash's identity compositionally. The richness of his skin is further highlighted by the contrast between his flesh tones and the yellows of the hat he is wearing, his bright red shirt collar and green-tinged cravat. Dash created the hat especially for the painting, making it out of sugar paper he found lying around. Its simple lines and tightness around his head recall the brimless, rounded shape of the black hat Gauguin wears in his own self-portrait – but the brightness of Dash's yellow hat serves to differentiate his identity from Gauguin's, and to declare a pride in his identity as a Black artist.

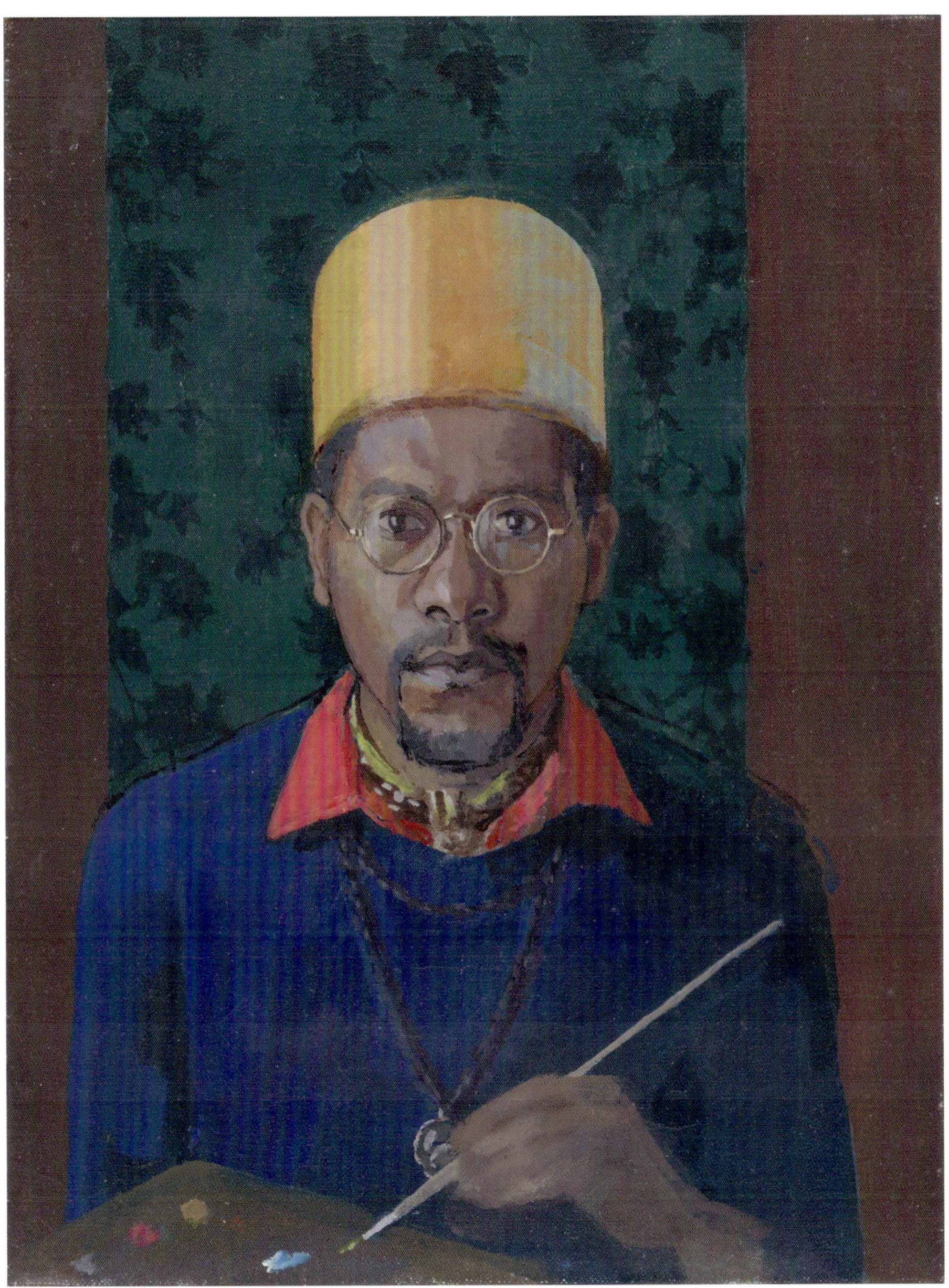

Robert Mapplethorpe 1946–89
Self Portrait 1980
Gelatin silver print on paper 35.2 × 35.2

Mapplethorpe stands squarely before the camera, his direct stare emphasising the kohl rims around his eyes and the mascara adorning his eyelashes. The light behind the camera falls from the right-hand side of the image, casting the left side of his face in shadow and creating a reflection on his mouth that emphasises the lip gloss he is wearing. Eye shadow wings out from the side of his eyes in a v shape, and powder contours his cheekbones against the bright glare of the studio light.

In addition to the make-up Mapplethorpe wears, the lighting and black-and-white nature of the photograph draw attention to the fur that surrounds his neck. In combination with the make-up, the fur collar (presumably attached to a coat) brings a sense of camp to the work. In her 1964 essay 'Notes on Camp', American theorist Susan Sontag listed 'women's clothes of the twenties' as being particularly camp, defining the term as follows:

> Camp sees everything in quotation marks. It's not a lamp, but a 'lamp'; not a woman, but a 'woman.' To perceive camp in objects and persons is to understand Being-as-Playing-a-Role. It is the farthest extension, in sensibility, of the metaphor of life as theater.

A definite sense of the performative pervades Mapplethorpe's self-portrait. The stark simplicity of the black-and-white image lends itself to the camp aesthetic, recalling Old Hollywood movie scenes. Within the chromatic binary of black and white, Mapplethorpe also disputes the veracity of a gender binary. Using make-up and fur coats, elements traditionally coded as feminine, Mapplethorpe performs a self that is neither traditionally male nor traditionally female. In the tradition of camp, Mapplethorpe presents 'Mapplethorpe'.

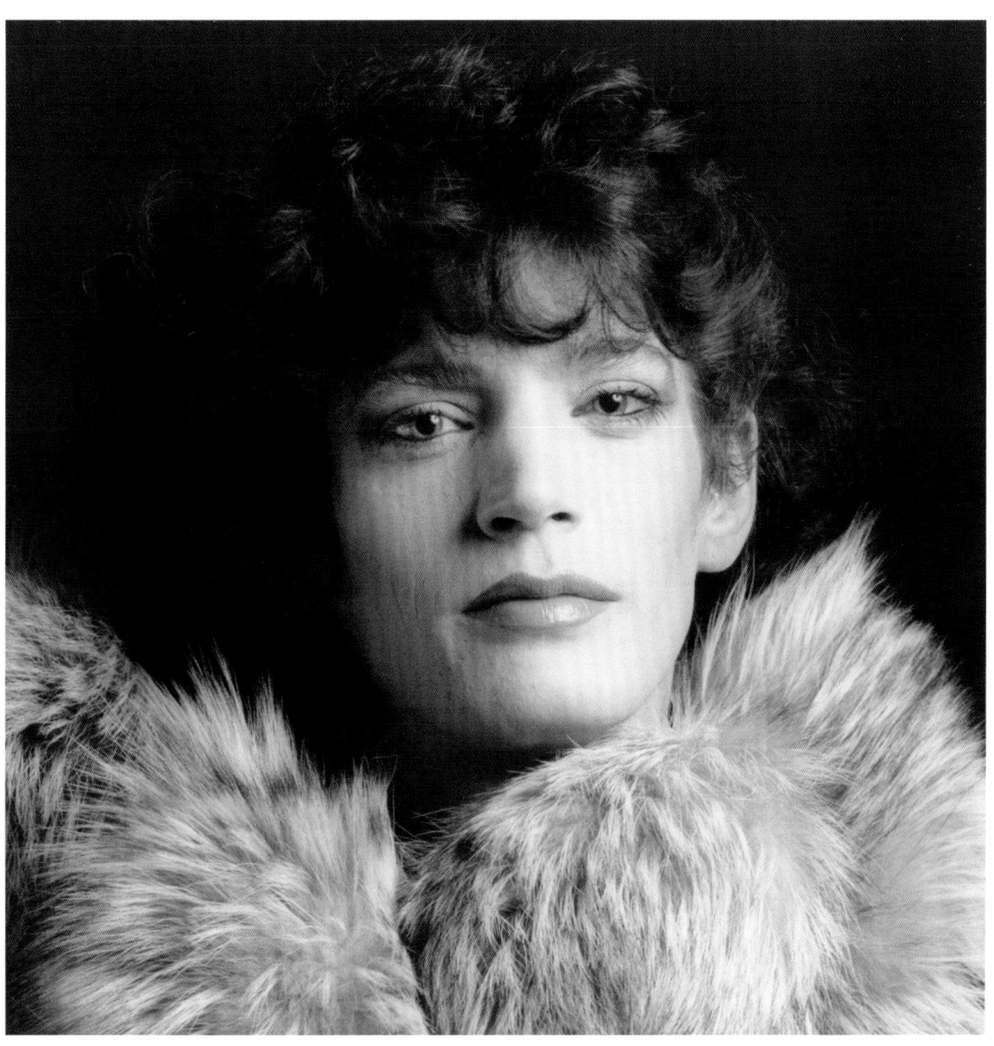

Andy Warhol 1928–87
Andy Warhol 1982
Lithograph on paper 108.2 × 74.9

Warhol used this image, originally taken as a snapshot by an unknown photographer, and turned it into multiple posters of himself. Warhol wears his trademark straight-haired, side-parted wig, which he started wearing as a means of disguising his early hair loss. Warhol started out with a platinum blonde wig, mimicking the colour of Marilyn Monroe's hair, before trading it in for a more avant-garde coloured one that teetered on the edge of platinum blonde and silver. Thereafter, Warhol was never seen out without a wig and it became a calling card of his artistic persona, not unlike Monroe's own artificial blonde hairstyle.

The embroidered-button jacket with its grandad collar looks as if Warhol may have simply purloined it from the cupboard of a local marching band. With the cheeky yet nonchalant air of his jacket and his sunglasses, Warhol is allying himself firmly with the New Romantics, a 1970s and 1980s fashion subculture that aimed to bring a glam rock twist to nineteenth-century Western Romanticism. The movement was deeply entwined with the underground club scene of major metropolitan cities like London and New York. In choosing to ally this image of himself as an artist with the movement, Warhol presents an idea of himself as a major figure in the nightlife of New York, where he lived at the time. In doing so, he suggests that his participation in the club scene is a key part of his artistic direction, a part of his creative process.

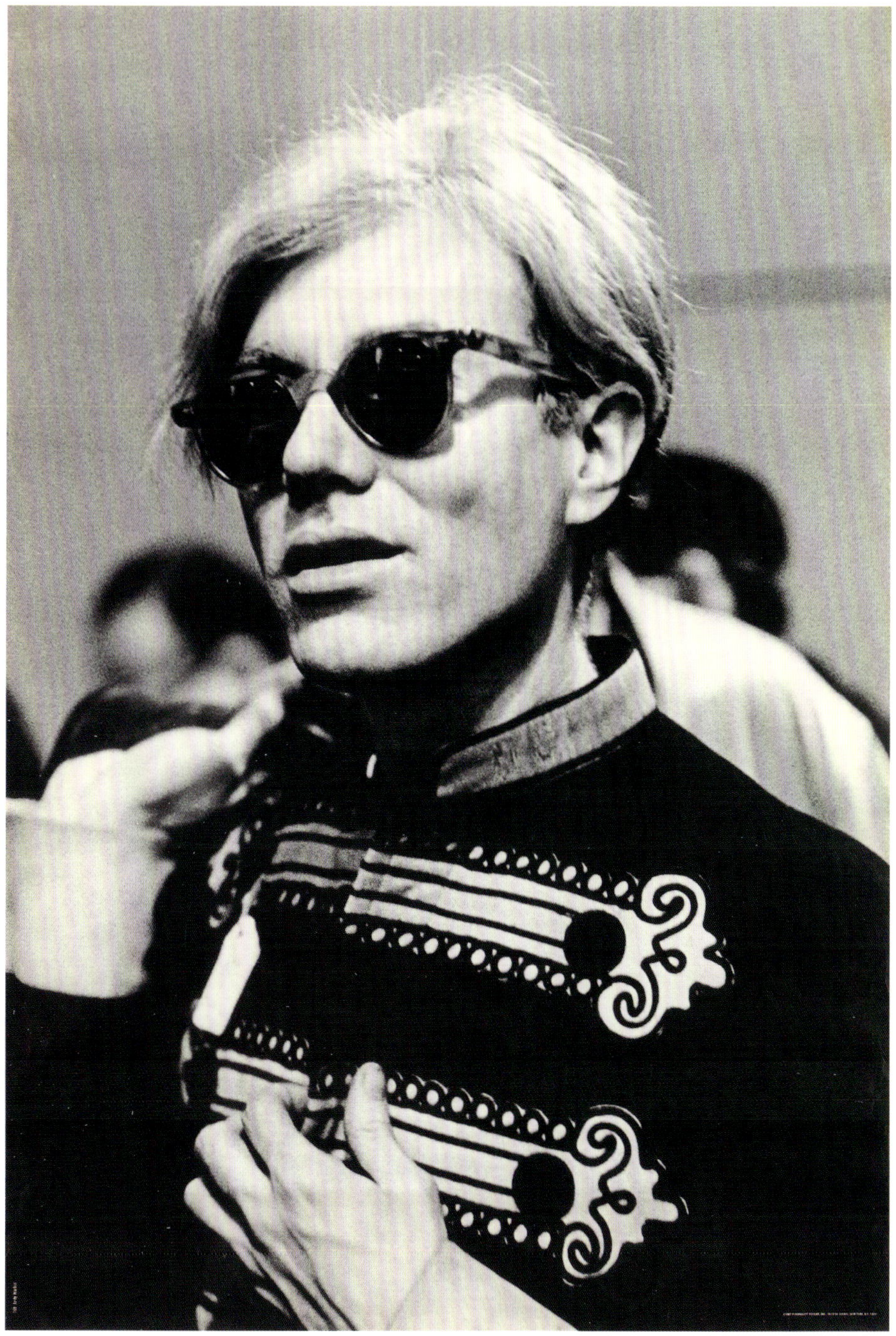

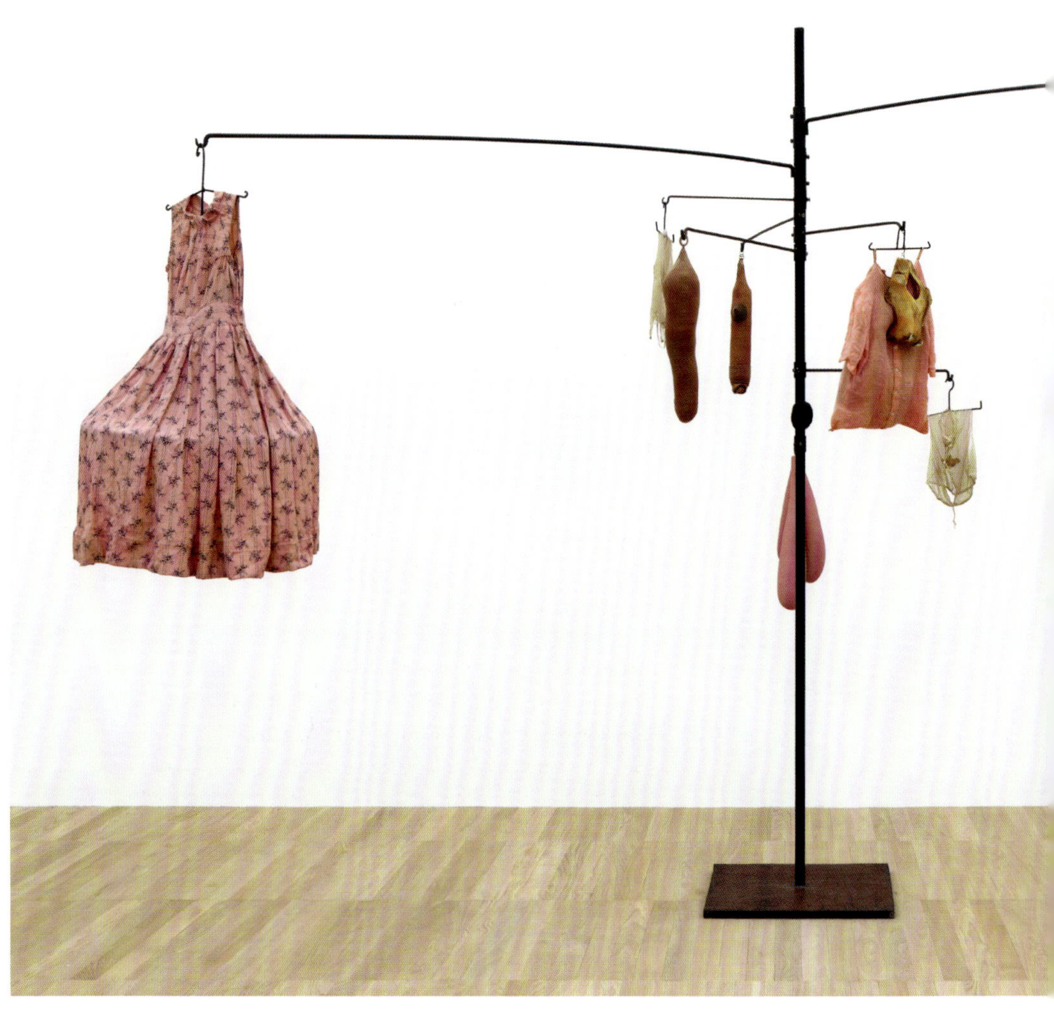

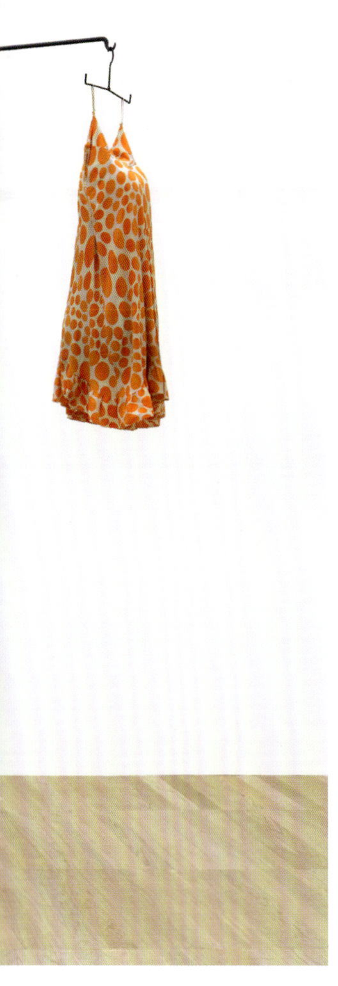

Louise Bourgeois 1911–2010
Untitled 1996
Clothing, rubber, steel and other materials
283.2 × 297.2 × 254 overall

During the 1990s, Bourgeois created a number of sculptures, in which she hung various garments on poles in the shape of a giant mobile. Bourgeois hangs her own clothes, past and present, as well as those of her mother, alongside a variety of small humanoid forms made from stuffed textiles. The different sizes, styles and conditions of the hanging garments suggests the different stages of life and the various roles women move between throughout their lives – daughter, wife, mother. The clothes are on hangers, discarded in a potentially radical gesture of rejection of these roles – or perhaps, more morbidly, indicating the natural outgrowth of them that comes from the progress towards inevitable death.

Bourgeois's piece relies on the current convention of dressing children and teenagers in distinct fashions, rather than in smaller versions of whatever happens to be in fashion for adults. This practice only came about in the sixteenth century. Clothing at this time lacked any gender, though, and the notion of dressing up 'as a little girl' only acquired meaning in the early twentieth century, when boys' clothing and girls' clothing began to be sold in department stores as separate categories. Girls were thus encouraged to act out their gender more explicitly, potentially becoming cognisant of the caregiver role and the daughter-wife-mother timeline earlier than they ever had before. Bourgeois's piece relies on this gendered garment evolution for its pathos and hints at a fatigued defeat on the part of the artist, who hangs these sartorial forms and their lifetime of gendered expectations on poles for the consumption of the viewer.

Sarah Lucas 1962–
Chicken Knickers 1997
Photograph on paper 42.6 × 42.6

In *Chicken Knickers*, Lucas photographs her lower torso and upper legs with an uncooked, headless whole chicken rested atop her genitalia. The chicken's rear rests precisely over the place where the artist's labia would be situated, and its opening echoes and draws attention to her sexual organs. Lucas is not naked, though. Beneath the raw and slightly bloody chicken she wears large, plain, white cotton knickers.

These knickers – with their large size, high waist and comfortably elasticated waistband – are colloquially known as 'granny pants', and are a style often favoured by those prioritising comfort over trends. In 1997, when Lucas created this work, Jean-Paul Gaultier presented runway looks that involved strappy revealing thongs showing from beneath layers of clothing, while at Gucci's Spring/Summer catwalk show, designer Tom Ford had models walking the runway in thongs alone on their lower halves. The trend for wearing thongs (and showing that one was wearing them, in a trend called a 'whale tale') grew exponentially. Thongs became synonymous with youthful, attractive women while, conversely, knickers became associated with those whom 1990s society deemed unattractive – the elderly. During this cultural moment, when a woman's choice of underwear was significantly high in the consciousness of those who follow major fashion houses and their runway shows, Lucas's choice is an act of defiance. Her placement of the chicken makes explicit reference to sex and sexiness, against the backdrop of a garment that had been deemed the opposite that very year.

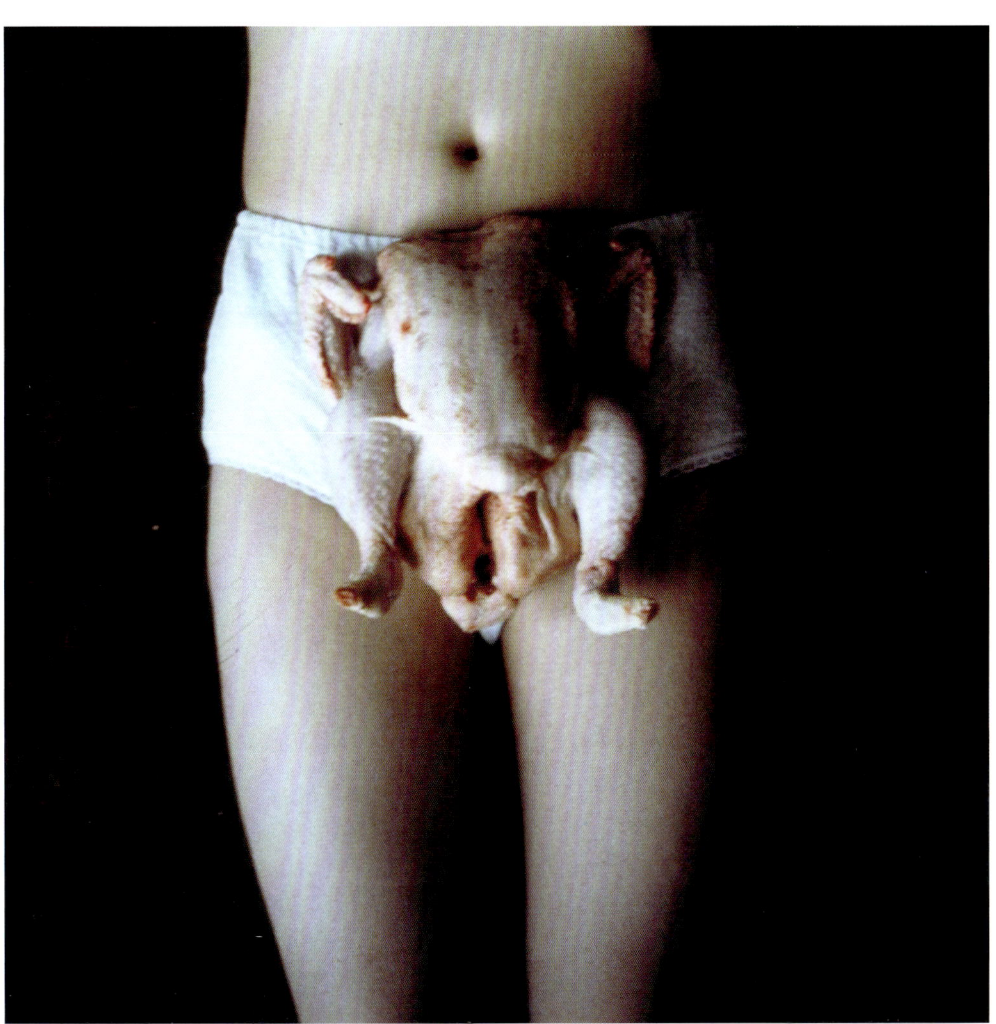

INDEX OF ARTISTS

NOTES

1 Honoré de Balzac, *Treatise on Elegant Living*, Cambridge, MA 2010 (first published 1830).

2 The full inscription on the image reads as follows:
'Rossetti, having just had a fresh consignment of "stunning" fabrics from that new shop in Regent Street, tries hard to prevail on his younger sister to accept at any rate one of these and have a dress made of it from designs to be furnished by himself.
D.G.R. "What is the use, Christina, of having a heart like a singing-bird and a water-shoot and all the rest of it, if you insist on getting yourself up like a pew-opener?"
C.R. (mildly) "Well, Gabriel, I don't know, I'm sure you yourself always dress very simply."'

3 Paul Bayley, Jon Savage, et al, *Linder: Works 1976–2006*, Zürich 2006, p.17.

4 This quote was included in Bohm's 2013 exhibition at Proud Galleries, curated by the artist's daughter, and presumably originates from an informal interview between Bohm and her daughter conducted in the lead up to the show.

CREDITS

Unless otherwise stated below, all photography © Tate, 2024
Front cover Copyright the Estate of Rose Finn-Kelcey. Courtesy the estate and Kate MacGarry, London
2 © Lubaina Himid, courtesy the artist and Hollybush Gardens, London
6 © Tate, 2024
12 © Njideka Akunyili Crosby. Commissioned by Art on the Underground
21 © Victoria and Albert Museum, London
23 Copyright of the Estate of Max Beerbohm
25 © ADAGP, Paris and DACS, London 2024
27 Collection: National Gallery of Modern Art, New Delhi. Courtesy The Estate of Vivan Sundaram
29 © Lubaina Himid, courtesy the artist and Hollybush Gardens, London
31 © Yinka Shonibare, courtesy Stephen Friedman Gallery, London
33 © Tania Bruguera
34–5 © Njideka Akunyili Crosby. Commissioned by Art on the Underground
36 © Chila Kumari Burman
43 Philadelphia Museum of Art, Pennsylvania, PA, USA / Gift of Ettie Stettheimer / Bridgeman Images
45 Estate of Nina Hamnett. All Rights Reserved 2024 / Bridgeman Images
49 © Claes Oldenburg
51 © James Barnor
53 © The Paolozzi Foundation, Licensed by DACS 2024
55 © Linder
57 © Jason Evans
59 © Chila Kumari Burman
61 © Amy Sherald. Courtesy the artist and Hauser & Wirth. National Portrait Gallery, Smithsonian Institution. Courtesy of the Smithsonian's National Portrait Gallery
64 © Estate of Edith Tudor-Hart
73 © Estate of Sylvia Pankhurst
75 © The estate of Augustus John. All Rights Reserved 2024 / Bridgeman Images
79 © The estate of Edith Tudor-Hart
81 © The Estate of Diane Arbus
83 © Estate of Jeanloup Sieff
85 © Estate of Paula Rego
87 Martin Parr / Magnum Photos / Photography (C) Tate, 2024 / Joe Humphrys
89 © Zanele Muholi
90 © The estate of Pauline Boty
92 © David Hockney
95 © Peter Blake 2024. All rights reserved, DACS
97 © The McNish Trust
99 © The estate of Pauline Boty
101 © Bridget Riley 2020. All rights reserved.
103 Albert and David Maysles © Yoko Ono / Photograph courtesy the artist
105 © Dorothy Bohm Estate
107 © The estate of Richard Hamilton
109 © David Hockney
110 Fondation Henri Cartier-Bresson / Magnum Photos
112 Chris Steele-Perkins / Magnum Photos
115 © Estate Brassaï – RMN-Grand Palais Localisation: Paris, fonds Gilberte Brassaï Photo © RMN-Grand Palais / Brassaï
117 Fondation Henri Cartier-Bresson / Magnum Photos
119 Copyright 2024 Neil Kenlock
121 © Sirkka-Liisa Konttinen. Courtesy the artist
123 © Estate of Al Vandenberg
125 © Karen Knorr and Olivier Richon
127 Mario De Biasi – Mondadori Portfolio
129 Chris Steele-Perkins / Magnum Photos
131 Martine Franck / Magnum Photos
132 © Keith Arnatt Estate. All rights reserved. DACS/Artimage 2024
134 © Paul Dash
139 © Estate of Vanessa Bell. All rights reserved, DACS 2024
141 © Tate, 2024
143 © Keith Arnatt Estate. All rights reserved. DACS/Artimage 2024
144–5 Copyright the Estate of Rose Finn-Kelcey. Courtesy the estate and Kate MacGarry, London
147 © Cindy Sherman. Courtesy the artist and Hauser & Wirth
149 © Paul Dash
151 © Robert Mapplethorpe Foundation
153 © 2024 The Andy Warhol Foundation for the Visual Arts, Inc. / Licensed by DACS, London
154–5 © The Easton Foundation/ VAGA at ARS, NY and DACS, London 2024
157 © Sarah Lucas.

The publishers have made every effort to trace the copyright holders of the works illustrated and apologise for any omissions or errors that may have been made.

First published 2024 by order of the Tate Trustees
by Tate Publishing, a division of Tate Enterprises Ltd,
Millbank, London SW1P 4RG
www.tate.org.uk/publishing

A catalogue record for this book is available from the British Library

ISBN 978 1 84976 838 2

Distributed in the United States and Canada by ABRAMS, New York

Library of Congress Control Number applied for

Senior Editor: Emma Poulter
Production: Roanne Marner
Picture Researcher: Emma O'Neill
Designed by Sandra Zellmer
Colour reproduction by DL Imaging Ltd, London
Printed and bound in Italy by Printer Trento S.r.l.

Front cover: Rose Finn-Kelcey *The Restless Image: a discrepancy between the felt position and the seen position* 1975 (detail, see pp.144–5)
Frontispiece: Lubaina Himid *Between the Two my Heart is Balanced* 1991 (detail, see p.29)
Page 4: Johan Zoffany *Colonel Blair with his Family and an Indian Ayah* 1786 (detail, see p.17)

Measurements of artworks are given in centimetres, height before width and depth

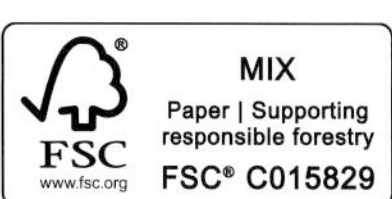